NEW PERSPECTIVES ON THE PAST

General Editor
R.I. Moore

Advisory Editors
Gerald Aylmer
Tanya Luhrmann
David Turley
Patrick Wormald

PUBLISHED

IN PREPARATION

By Eugene Kamenka

The Ethical Foundations of Marxism
Marxism and Ethics
The Philosophy of Ludwig Feuerbach
The Portable Karl Marx

Edited by Eugene Kamenka

A World in Revolution?: The University Lectures 1970
Paradigm for Revolution? The Paris Commune 1871–1971
Nationalism – The Nature and Evolution of an Idea
Feudalism, Capitalism and Beyond (with R.S. Neale)
Law and Society – The Crisis in Legal Ideals (with Robert Brown and
A.E.-S. Tay)
Human Rights (with A.E.-S. Tay)
Bureaucracy: The Career of a Concept (with Martin Krygier)
Law and the Future of Society (with F.C. Hutley and A.E.-S. Tay)
Intellectuals and Revolution – Socialism and the Experience of 1848 (with
F.B. Smith)
Justice (with A.E.-S. Tay)
Law-Making in Australia (with A.E.-S. Tay)
Law and Social Control (with A.E.-S. Tay)
Community as a Social Ideal
Utopias

BUREAUCRACY

Eugene Kamenka

Basil Blackwell

First published 1989

Basil Blackwell Ltd
108 Cowley Road, Oxford, OX4 1JF, UK

Basil Blackwell Inc.
3 Cambridge Center,
Cambridge, Massachusetts 02142, USA

British Library Cataloguing in Publication Data

A CIP catalogue record for this book is available
from the British Library.

Library of Congress Cataloging in Publication Data
Kamenka, Eugene.
    Bureaucracy / Eugene Kamenka.
        p.   cm. — (New perspectives on the past)
    Bibliography: p.
    Includes index.
    ISBN 0–631–14578–8 — ISBN 0–631–14579–6 (pbk.)
    1. Bureaucracy—History.   I. Title.   II. Series: New perspectives
on the past (Basil Blackwell Publisher)
JF1341.K35   1989
350′.001—dc20   89–34522
                                                                        CIP

The quotation on pp. 23–5 of this book is taken from Etienne Balazs *Chinese Civilization and Bureaucracy: Variations on a Theme* trans. H. M. Wright (New Haven, Yale, 1964) and is reproduced by permission of Yale University Press.

Typeset in 10½ on 12pt Plantin
by Footnote Graphics, Warminster, Wilts.
Printed in Great Britain by
Billing & Sons, Ltd.

Contents

Editor's Preface

Ignorance has many forms, and all of them are dangerous. In the nineteenth and twentieth centuries our chief effort has been to free ourselves from tradition and superstition in large questions, and from the error in small ones upon which they rest, by redefining the fields of knowledge and evolving in each the distinctive method appropriate for its cultivation. The achievement has been incalculable, but not without cost. As each new subject has developed a specialist vocabulary to permit rapid and precise reference to its own common and rapidly growing stock of ideas and discoveries, and come to require a greater depth of expertise from its specialists, scholars have been cut off by their own erudition not only from mankind at large, but from the findings of workers in other fields, and even in other parts of their own. Isolation diminishes not only the usefulness but the soundness of their labours when energies are exclusively devoted to eliminating the small blemishes so embarrassingly obvious to the fellow-professional on the next patch, instead of avoiding others that may loom much larger from, as it were, a more distant vantage point. Marc Bloch observed a contradiction in the attitudes of many historians: 'when it is a question of ascertaining whether or not some human act has really taken place, they cannot be too painstaking. If they proceed to the reasons for that act, they are content with the merest appearance, ordinarily founded upon one of those maxims of common-place psychology which are neither more nor less true than their opposites.' When the historian peeps across the fence he sees his neighbours, in literature, perhaps, or sociology, just as complacent in relying on historical platitudes which are naive, simplistic or obsolete.

New Perspectives on the Past represents not a reaction against specialization, which would be a romantic absurdity, but an attempt to come to terms with it. The authors, of course, are specialists, and their thought and conclusions rest on the foundation of distinguished professional research in different periods and fields. Here they will free themselves, as far as it is possible,

from the constraints of subject, region and period within which
they ordinarily and necessarily work, to discuss problems simply
as problems, and not as 'history' or 'politics' or 'economics'.
They will write for specialists, because we are all specialists now,
and for laymen, because we are all laymen.

From Mesopotamia to the modern state the history of complex
societies is, before it can be anything else, a history of organization – of how and by whom, on what conditions and with what
results, force is summoned, taxes gathered, payments and rewards distributed. Writing itself was invented to keep track of
tribute delivered to the temples of Sumer, reflecting a transition
from more or less arbitrary demands to fixed and regular – and
doubtless much more lucrative – payments, with all that that
entailed for the daily rhythms both of the peasant who produced
the goods and of the priests who stored and used them. As a
phenomenon bureaucracy is at the very basis of civilization and
its development; as a concept it is fundamental to social thought.
The immense span of world history which Eugene Kamenka
brings under review in this short book demonstrates the dependence of human achievement and its character on the ways in
which power is mobilized and directed. His remarkable clarity
exemplifies at the same time the power of the idea itself as a
principle of historical analysis. Yet just because of the usefulness
of the idea and the enormous variety of its applications, bureaucracy has become a much abused word, as well as one which is
surrounded by a body of rich but often complex and unapproachable theoretical discussion. Working historians, at all levels, will
be as grateful for Kamenka's concise and businesslike approach
to the problems that result as theorists will be for the wide range
of historical material he places at their disposal with such
liveliness and lucidity.

R. I. Moore

Preface

The spread and increasing power of bureaucracy – in part the massively accelerated growth of large-scale, centralized administrative structures – is one of the most noticed and discussed phenomena of our time. The concept – still vaguely defined and not all that well analysed – cuts across the distinctions between capitalism and communism, democracy and dictatorship, the industrialized 'Western world' and the organized despotisms of ancient empires and 'agro-managerial' societies. It bids fair to dominate our future, but it has also shaped our past. The concept 'bureaucracy' is as important as its uses are varied, unexamined and confused.

John Davey and Bob Moore were kind enough to invite me to write this book. I owe them much for persuading me to return to grappling with a phenomenon that is fascinating and difficult. I have, no doubt, done it less than justice, but I have learnt a great deal in the attempt. Perhaps the reader will find the same.

I also owe much to the excellent conditions for research and writing hitherto offered by the Institute of Advanced Studies of the Australian National University. I have now worked in its History of Ideas Unit for a quarter of a century, and continue to rejoice in the stimulation gained from colleagues and visitors there. One of the Unit's former PhD students, Martin Krygier, now Associate Professor of Law in the University of New South Wales, worked in the Unit on Marxism and bureaucracy; he co-edited with me and wrote four of the six chapters in *Bureaucracy: The Career of a Concept* (London, 1979). My debt to him is considerable. Another, Marian Sawer, had completed and published her examination of *Marxism and the Question of the Asiatic Mode of Production* (The Hague, 1977). Yet another, David Lovell, now of the Department of Government in the Australian Defence Forces Academy and the University of New South Wales, revised, in the course of other work in the Unit, his critical essay *Trotsky's Analysis of Soviet Bureaucratization*, (London, 1985). I have learnt much from them, from my Unit colleague Robert Brown and from other colleagues in Canberra and the Australian National University who have worked on bureaucracy or related topics: Brian Beddie, Eva Etzioni-Halevy, Oliver MacDonagh, R.F. Miller and T.H. Rigby, not to speak of such visitors as K.A. Wittfogel, Maximilien Rubel, Shlomo Avineri, S.N. Eisenstadt, Baruch Knei-Paz, Ken Minogue, George Mosse, Peter Self, Melvin Richter and George Feaver. Elizabeth Short, for this book as for so many of the others I have written or edited, has collected materials, checked references, read proofs and compiled an index. Hong Li-Jian, now working in the History of Ideas Unit on the 'Asiatic Mode of Production' in Chinese historiography and Marxist debate in modern China, has helped me survey writing on the origin and development of ancient Chinese bureaucracy. The General Editor of this series, Bob Moore, and Gerald Aylmer have been kind enough to comment on drafts of this book; they have sought to save me from many errors and infelicities. Vibeke Wetselaar and Wendie Hare have coped with constant changes to the typescript with their usual but nevertheless remarkable cheerfulness.

For some years, Alice Tay and I have been engaged in exploring Marxist conceptions and critiques of law and legal theory – in Western Marxist writing, in the USSR and Eastern Europe and in the People's Republic of China. In the process, we have been led to a more sustained grappling with the relationship and distinction between law and administration and between what we call *Gemeinshaft, Gesellschaft* and bureaucratic-administrative conceptions of society, law and government. In writing this book, I have again drawn on much of our joint work and on what I have learnt through my participation in it and in thirty years of exciting and happy living and talking together.

The University of British Columbia in Vancouver was kind enough, in the last third of 1986, to invite me to its Department of Political Science. It was there that I finished the first draft of this book. For the hospitality offered and the stimulation gained, I am grateful to Professor David Elkins, head of that department, Professor Peter Burns, Dean of the Faculty of Law, Professor J.C. Smith and their many colleagues, who also became mine.

Eugene Kamenka
Canberra

And it came to pass on the morrow, that Moses sat to judge the people: and the people stood by Moses from the morning unto the evening.

And when Moses' father in law [Jethro the priest of Midian] saw all that he did to the people, he said, What is this thing that thou doest to the people? why sittest thou thyself alone, and all the people stand by thee from morning unto even?

And Moses said unto his father in law, Because the people come unto me to enquire of God:

When they have a matter, they come unto me; and I judge between one and another, and I do make them know the statutes of God, and his laws.

And Moses' father in law said unto him, The thing that thou doest is not good.

Thou wilt surely wear away, both thou, and this people that is with thee: for this thing is too heavy for thee; thou art not able to perform it thyself alone.

Hearken now unto my voice, I will give thee counsel, and God shall be with thee: Be thou for the people to God-ward, that thou mayest bring the causes unto God:

And thou shalt teach them ordinances and laws, and shalt shew them the way wherein they must walk, and the work that they must do.

Moreover thou shalt provide out of all the people able men, such as fear God, men of truth, hating covetousness; and place such over them, to be rulers of thousands, and rulers of hundreds, rulers of fifties, and rulers of tens:

And let them judge the people at all seasons: and it shall be, that every great matter they shall bring unto thee, but every small matter they shall judge: so shall it be easier for thyself, and they shall bear the burden with thee.

If thou shalt do this thing, and God command thee so, then thou shalt be able to endure, and all this people shall also go to their place in peace.

So Moses hearkened to the voice of his father in law, and did all that he had said.

Exodus XVIII, 13–24

1
Ancient Bureaucracies

Administration – ancient and modern

The study of bureaucracy, at least under that name, is a modern phenomenon. Yet administration as an institutionalized activity has been carried out in stratified, complex societies since very early times. Some of those ancient societies, indeed, were among the most intensively and systematically administered societies known to mankind.

The great father figure of the modern theory of bureaucracies, the German sociologist Max Weber (1864–1920), himself studied ancient systems of government and their sophisticated administrative arrangements and staffs. Nevertheless, he distinguished sharply between them and modern 'rational' bureaucracies. Ancient bureaucracies were linked with and depended upon a patrimonial ruler, originally the father of his people, whose *oikos* or household has become large and diffuse, but who still claims loyalty and respect as its indispensable head. His powers are legitimate in so far as they are paternalistic and traditional and his great domains are still seen as extensions of his household. The office that is patrimonial in origin or authority lacks any separation of the private and the official sphere. Political administration is treated as a personal affair of the ruler, even if in the larger society he must exercise it through others. Pure or 'ideal-type' bureaucracy, for Weber, in contrast, is depersonalized, rationalistic, rule-bound behaviour ordered by laws and administrative regulations. It separates the bureau from the private domicile of the official; it divorces official activity from the sphere of private pursuits and attitudes. It demands of the bureaucrat a 'vocation' – allegiance not to a person but to the purpose of his office and the rules laid down for its activities. For Weber, therefore, ancient societies and more recent traditional ones may develop bureaucratic features but fully fledged 'rational' bureaucracy and bureaucratic institutions come into their own only with the development of rationalism, of the modern state and of the money economy.

Weber's writing on bureaucracy, like his classic *Wirtschaft und Gesellschaft* in which it is embedded, appears to be more systematic and conceptually ordered than it is. He used, but was fundamentally suspicious of, universal descriptive concepts. It was on that basis that he spoke of bureaucracies both in the ancient world and in the modern. More apposite for social science, however, according to Weber, was the notion of an *ideal type*. This was neither an empirical average nor a set of general features to be found in every institution of that sort. It was, rather, a paradigm – a mixture of arrangements, presuppositions and beliefs standing in a relationship of mutual reinforcement with each other, capable of development into a coherent system. Central to Weber's conception of rational bureaucracy, the bureaucracy of the modern world as the only pure, ideal-type bureaucracy, was Weber's belief that earlier, patrimonial and traditional bureaucracies were inherently unstable, incapable of coherent development. They were unstable, he thought, because in the absence of impersonality and of a fully developed money economy, offices readily became fiefs. Officials left to pay themselves out of the taxes they collected or the product of the lands and activities they administered became or tended to become independent. The system threatened to fragment. The bureaucratic centre, and especially the ruler, lost control over the periphery.[1]

'The type of organization designed to accomplish large-scale administrative tasks by systematically coordinating the work of many individuals is called a bureaucracy', Peter M. Blau writes in one of the more interesting contributions to the subject.[2] Such bureaucracies belong to the class of formal organizations, as distinct from informal groupings, in so far as they are engaged in pursuing explicit announced objectives through manifestly coordinated efforts. These definitions, like Weber's discussion of bureaucracy, reveal or emphasize a *functionalist* approach. They see bureaucracy as performing a social *task*. They see it, too, as a

---

1   Max Weber, *Economy and Society: An Outline of Interpretive Sociology*, ed. Guenther Roth and Claus Wittich, 3 vols, New York, 1968, pp. 215–66 and 1006–110.
2   Peter M. Blau, *Bureaucracy in Modern Society*, New York, 1956, p. 14.

form of imperative coordination, as a way of structuring and coordinating commands given from the top, of ensuring that they will be obeyed and of assembling and evaluating information gained from below.

It is not necessary, in speaking functionally, to argue that the function of an organization precedes the emergence of that organization in history – that the organization is constructed or consciously designed according to a prior blueprint. Neither need one claim that the function is an essence of which all other features of the organization are manifestations. Functions can and do evolve. Those who become carriers of the function may have earlier or simultaneous unrelated claims to obedience and authority, not always extinguished by their new functional role. The function therefore does not determine or exhaustively describe all the features of an organization. The point is rather that the function becomes a relatively central consideration, striving to determine goals, internal structure, criteria of performance and accounting for much of the social respect accorded to the institution. It is in the light of this that Weber constructed his ideal type, against which any historical bureaucracy is to be judged as central-function-efficient or not and in the light of which, other, non-bureaucratic, roles or attitudes may appear incompatible, disruptive of bureaucratic institutions as pure 'ideal-type' bureaucracies.

For Weber coordination in a bureaucracy, aiming above all at efficiency, takes place on the basis of an *impersonal, hierarchical structure of authority* and a *centrally controlled and supervised delegation of functions*. Federalism, the limited but real independence of feudalism and even the collegial principle of organization which dominated seventeenth-century German public administration, for instance, thus come into conflict with the bureaucratic principle, with bureaucracy as an 'ideal type'. For in bureaucracy, the command structure is unified, not fragmented. A true bureaucrat is free to act only in so far as he is empowered to do so and in the light of bureaucratic procedures and specified goals, while a feudal lord is free to do all that which he is not specifically forbidden to do.

The authority which a bureaucracy serves, the ruler who dictates its goals, is not – Weber insisted – part of the bureaucracy, but stands above it and outside it. The bureaucracy itself is a *specialized administrative staff*, trained to perform specific tasks and to act within the powers delegated to it or ascribed to each particular office. It tends to develop an *esprit de corps*, which includes a sense of *vocation. Rewards* within the bureaucracy are *differentiated according to office* but also made conditional upon satisfactory performance. The failure to develop such staffs, Weber believed, accounted for the fleeting character of some great and otherwise complex African empires.

Central to Weber's conception of social rule and administration was his insistence that abiding social authority rested on or required legitimacy and a marked degree of cooperation. There had to be a widespread belief of the ruled that the ruler had the right to issue commands and to be obeyed. This was *Herrschaft* – legitimate sovereignty and not mere coercion or domination. Weber's central social distinction was not between bureaucratic societies and non-bureaucratic societies, but between three pure or ideal types of legitimate authority on which *Herrschaft* could be based. He set these out in a famous passage of *Wirtschaft und Gesellschaft. Traditional authority* rested on an established belief in the sanctity of immemorial tradition and the legitimacy of status of those who exercised authority under these traditions. *Charismatic authority* arose on the basis of the specific and exceptional sanctity, heroism or exemplary character of an individual person and from the normative patterns or order revealed or ordained by him. *Rational authority* in contrast rested on a legally established impersonal order which endowed holders of an office with the formal legal power to issue commands as long as they acted *intra vires*. It was this last kind of authority that was for Weber a modern phenomenon.

Weber recognized, of course, that charisma could become 'routinized' by heredity or by ritual and thus pass through prescribed procedures to successors. Traditional and charismatic authority could become mixed; concrete historical reality could not be exhausted in a conceptual scheme of ideal types.

Using the word bureaucracy in its more general sense, Weber singled out several historical examples of rather distinctly developed and quantitatively large bureaucracies that existed before the modern period. These were those of Egypt in the period of the New Kingdom, of the later Roman Principate, the Dominate and the Byzantine polity that developed out of it, of the Roman Catholic Church, especially from the end of the thirteenth century, and of the scholar-administrators in China, central to Chinese government from China's unification under the Qin more than 2,000 years ago. But all of these, for Weber, contained not only patrimonial but also prebendal or feudal elements, resting on compensation to officials in kind, and therefore failing to assure the permanence of their structures and of the centre's control.

Guy Benveniste has modern bureaucracies (and Weber) in mind when he writes

> there is a universal culture of organizations that transcends political or economic ideologies of the left or of the right ... control, rewards, punishment, careers, promotions, corruption, errors and fear exist anywhere modern bureaucratic structures are established ... there is a universal culture of organizations that stresses task orientation and goal attainment (making a profit or fulfilling plan objectives) ... which emphasizes what is systematic, thorough and painstaking; which endorses verification, control and formalization; which rejects amusement, pleasure, and delight for their own sake; which applauds risk-taking but rarely encourages it; which rejects hedonism in the organization as sheer fantasy; which assumes that organizational survival is the only relevant goal to be pursued.[3]

In this chapter, we shall endeavour to bring out that even such features have a longer history than Weber willingly admitted. They go back to the early history of civilization, to the first major states. They were not only displayed but discussed by bureaucrats more than 2,000 years ago – most consistently, perhaps, in China even before the unification of the empire under the Qin and Former Han dynasties in the third century BC. However, we find similar discussions in the India of the Mauryas and traces of highly sophisticated administrative complexities in Sumer, Babylon and the Egypt of the Old and Middle Kingdoms. In the New Kingdom of Egypt, Egyptian bureaucratic administration was at its most developed, capable of serving as a model for subsequent empires in the West and Middle East.

3 Guy Benveniste, *Bureaucracy*, San Francisco, 1977, p. xv.

The formation of states

Cities and city-states emerged, so far as we know at present, in Mesopotamia soon after the Sumerian conquest of 3500 BC. They represent the culmination of a cultural development already evident in hamlets of the preceding Ubaidian culture. By 3000 BC these cities were witnessing remarkable developments in art and architecture, in social organization and administration, in religious thought and practice. Many scholars, perhaps most, believe that the experience and prosperity brought by extensive irrigation lay at the basis of these developments. The Sumerians had already taken the first steps in the invention of writing, again possibly on a pre-Sumerian base. They were evolving from a democratic political system of town councils and public (city) ownership of land on behalf of its god to kingship, inter-urban warfare and the formation of proto-empires. Specialized but not necessarily hereditary castes responsible for the ordering and maintenance of social relationships, the collection of taxes, the erection of temples and public works and the distribution and redistribution of goods and resources emerged with surprising rapidity. They owed their allegiance or authority to god or king, or to god–king. They helped to maintain a fundamental correspondence and harmony between society and the cosmos, between this world and the other world. But in the process, they carried out a large variety of practical tasks – initiating, administering, supervising, controlling and verifying. Together with the ruler, they came to constitute the *centre* – political, cultural, religious – from which authority flowed and on which the cohesion of the wider society was based.

Hand in hand with this development went increasing division of labour, differentiation of rank, caste and class and the ever-greater scope and importance of public works, public activities and public concerns, including war and, in the Euphrates and Nile valleys, further flood control and irrigation. Rulers became more clearly differentiated from the rest of society and more powerful. Around the person or 'office' of such rulers – often combining religious, military and political functions – a state and state apparatus developed, sometimes encouraging and merging with a complex religious and priestly apparatus, sometimes in tension and competition with it. Regional and functional loyalties and associations came to supersede kinship; loyalty to the 'centre' became increasingly important. As the territories and responsibilities of particular rulers expanded so did their administrative staffs. The word 'state', however, has to be used under *caveat* in this context. The word itself, coined by Machiavelli, and many of its associations are comparatively modern. The early state was not distinguished from the person of the ruler or, at all sharply, from the city or the country and its god, from the requirements of the polity or the governance of heaven. The Greek concept of '*polis*' and the Roman '*res publica*' stand closer to it but in Mesopotamia and Egypt, in India and China, both the state and the empire or country were unthinkable without its god or gods and, then, without the ruler and his special relationship with a cosmic order and the god or gods that sustained it.

The development of bureaucratic power, at least in its broad sense as the rule of officials, and of bureaucratic castes in history, is an integral part of this emergence of the state and of the powerful ruler. The state in turn has been the most visible carrier and developer of bureaucratic organization and power. These became most evident in those great near-eastern and oriental states that were believed to have practised large-scale irrigation and flood control since early times. A number of eighteenth- and nineteenth-century thinkers, including Marx, saw such bureaucratized state-centred despotisms as arising on the basis of great public works and the political unimportance of private property. Only more recently have there been historically informed attempts to trace the origin of the state, or of states, generally. There is widespread agreement, of course, with the Marxist insistence, succinctly formulated by Engels in his *Origin of the Family, Private Property and the State* (1884) that 'the state . . . has not existed from all eternity. There have been societies which have managed without it, which had no notion of the state or state power'.[4] His conclusion that, at a definite stage of economic development which necessarily involved the cleavage of society into classes, the state became a necessity because of this cleavage, has been more controversial. In *The Origin of the Family* Engels elevated his best known but crudest account of the origin of the

4   F. Engels, *The Origin of the Family, Private Property and the State*, London, 1972, p. 232.

state as rooted in the enforcement and maintenance of class privilege and economic exploitation in the interest of a ruling class. In his *Anti-Dühring* (1877–8) he emphasized rather a gradual change of 'functional' power into 'exploitative' power, in which the servant of the community gradually became the overlord and the tribal chiefs of primitive society were transformed into the rulers of class society. In both versions Engels stressed the role of military force, of war and conquest (allegedly resulting in the institution of slavery), as crucial in the rise of the state. Like most nineteenth-century rationalists, he had no feeling for the role of religion in the formation of societies. Marx in the study of pre-capitalist formations he undertook in the 1850s (part of the *Grundrisse*) put less weight on war or class conflict. He reached the conclusion that, for important parts of the world at least, the exploitation of producers living in village communities was not based on the existence of private ownership of land but, rather, or at least mostly, on allegiance to the deified and despotic ruler who personified the state. There thus arose the dichotomy and mutual interdependence between agricultural communities and state organizations brought into being by the need for constructing and maintaining irrigation systems, on a scale beyond the capacities of the village community itself.

For the past fifty years, especially, the rise and character of the early state has been the subject of increasingly informed, but never totally resolved, debate.[5] Some agree with Morton H. Fried, who argued in his *The Evolution of Political Society* (1967) that political society generally evolves from an egalitarian community to one with ranks, then to the stratified community where strata have unequal access to the basic resources that sustain life, and finally to a state society. The function of the state is to maintain, by force, unequal access to basic resources. This is possible only when there is a significant surplus, built up through the division of labour. Others, on the other hand, emphasize much more strongly the religious foundations of rule and kingship and their independent force or, at a more material level, the origin of the state in conquest, in the need to administer new and alien territories where custom and tradition, let alone democratic

---

5 In the summary of recent opinions that follows I draw on Henri J.M. Claessen and Peter Skalník, 'The Early State: Theories and Hypotheses', in Claessen and Skalnik, eds, *The Early State*, The Hague, 1978, pp. 3–29.

assembly, would not serve. But all would concede that initial appropriation and use or redistribution of social surplus is a central function of the states that arise. There is more disagreement on the specific conditions that bring states and bureaucracies into being and on the functions with which they justify their existence. A careful analysis of the work of Marx and Engels, even, shows that their detailed accounts were never mono-causal, but brought in a number of distinct factors as necessary for that development. Factors now emphasized are increase in population, the growing complexity of the division of labour, especially with urbanization and the expansion of trade, the impact of war and defence, or even of the threat of war, and the increasing stratification of society as a result of all of these. Some stress internal exploitation and tax collection; others put more weight on military ambitions and activities and the need to administer conquered territories; others again still emphasize public works, especially irrigation and flood control. Some are more comfortable than others with the religious functions and foundations of state rule, with the role played by the king as maintainer of an order that is at once cosmic and social, and with the importance and elaborate organization of sacrifice and temple worship, as well as of a system of justice and law.

V. Gordon Childe's approach is still influential though increasingly criticized by those who reject evolutionary models and the use of the state as a yardstick of progress. Childe connected the origin of the state specifically with the urban revolution in human society that took place some 5,000 years ago (though the Egypt of the Old Kingdom, it is generally held, developed a state but no important urban centres). Childe listed the following important factors:

1 *Size* – an increase in settlement size toward urban proportions.
2 *The existence of a surplus* and the centralized accumulation of capital through the imposition of tribute and taxation.
3 *Monumental public works.*
4 The invention of *writing*.
5 The *elaboration* of exact and predictive *sciences*.
6 The appearance and growth of *long-distance trade* in luxuries.
7 The emergence of a *class-stratified society* based on unequal distribution of social surplus.

8   The composition and function of an *urban centre*, freeing
    part of the population from full-time subsistence tasks for
    full-time craft specialization.
9   The state as an organization based on *residence rather than
    kinship*.

Others – L. White, J.H. Steward, E.R. Service and M.
Sahlins – fashioned the evolutionary ladder of band, tribe, chief
and state by looking at the organizing principles of ranking and
stratification, though Steward, like K.A. Wittfogel, insisted that
irrigation played a major role in producing a leap forward in
social organization, power and coordination which in the end led
to state formation. Some of their critics seem not so much
concerned to deny that these shifts took place – though in more
complex ways than a simple evolutionary scheme might suggest –
as to criticize the postulation of a steady increase in complexity
and the historical existence of an impasse of savagery to be
broken through. They elevate the nomad hunter: he knew about
agriculture, they say, but rejected a full-scale transition to it as
involving too much hard work without corresponding benefit –
until non-cultural external conditions (change in climate or in
population pressure?) forced him into agriculture.

Two recent students of the early state have concluded that it 'is
a centralized socio-political organization for the regulation of
social relations in a complex, stratified society divided into at
least two basic strata, or emergent social classes – viz. the rulers
and the ruled – whose relations are characterized by political
dominance of the former and tributary obligations of the latter,
legitimized by a common ideology of which reciprocity is the
basic principle'.[6] The criteria of central government having
legitimate power to enforce decisions, of the existence of a
separate group of rulers and of an ideology that legitimates this
specific form of government are, for them, sufficient to distinguish the early state from chiefdoms, ranked societies etc. They
highlight six factors as connected with the emergence and
subsequent development of the early state: population growth,
war, conquest, ideology, the production of a surplus and the
influence of already existing states. These factors, they argue,

6   Claessen and Skalník, op. cit., p. 640.

were mutually reinforcing; they produced a snowball effect which could work positively to make the state grow in size, power and complexity or negatively to reinforce decline or even collapse. In a later work, the ideological factor was given more emphasis while war and conquest were reduced to a secondary role as corollaries of economic or even possibly ideological competition. Some new variables – including irrigation and the role of trade – were pushed more strongly to the fore and dominance and control of the economy were treated as more primary than the extraction of a surplus. The authors insist that none of the factors involved could be selected as a prime mover; the strength of each varied in specific cases. It has also become fashionable to elaborate Edward Shils's centre–periphery analysis (discussed below) into a concept of central or supra-system dominance over continuing sub-systems or micro-networks of social relations that retain some autonomy. This differentiates states from bands and tribes and enables authors to explain the collapse of states by a failure in supra-system dominance.[7]

For those interested in the character and growth of bureaucracy, though, the growth of the state remains fundamental and the weight to be assigned to various factors in accounting for its origin surprisingly unimportant, except in providing backing for the rejection of essentialist and mono-causal explanation. The latter are easily exposed by simply recognizing that causality is a triadic and not a dyadic relation. It requires three, not two, terms. A single cause does not and cannot produce an effect by itself: it must act on something and only the interaction of at least two factors can produce a result that was not there before. Each of these factors or 'causes' is necessary; neither alone is sufficient. An overwhelming practical problem which complicates this analysis is provided by the fact that there are always far more than two factors that appear important and often, in a given situation, there is 'overdetermination' – that is, any one of a number of factors might have been sufficient to produce the result in that situation.

7 Henri J.M. Claessen and Pieter van de Velde, eds, *Early State Dynamics*, Leiden, 1987, passim, but especially in the Introduction and the contributions by Thomas Bargatzky and Patricia A. Shifferd. See also M.A. Vitkin, 'Marx and Weber on the Primary State', in H.J.M. Claessen and P. Skalník, eds, *The Study of the State*, The Hague, 1981, pp. 4 ` ` -54.

Ancient Mesopotamia

The early state and its ruler or rulers, in principle but also in practice, represented and took responsibility for public affairs, for those aspects of social, political, economic and religious life that extended beyond the interest and capacities of the village community and its still largely collective mode of agricultural production. States, generally, have arisen only after the transition to settled agricultural life, though there is now some dispute about this because some pastoral societies, e.g. in central Asia, have developed state structures in connection with war and regularized international trade with agricultural neighbours and because states have been founded and carried on by nomad conquerors. In ancient Mesopotamia, dominated by a series of city-led agriculturally based 'storage economies', the 'great organizations' of the temple and the king's household carried out industrial production on a much larger scale than villages or private households. They took responsibility, with or under the ruler, for the maintenance of public buildings and city ramparts and for public works. Officials had, periodically, to count and account for goods, staples and animals belonging to or dispatched by an authority. They collected or verified the collection of taxes and tributes, organized *corvée* labour, supervised military service obligations, recorded the yield of royal or priestly domains and workshops and oversaw the distribution of materials and rations to craftsmen and workers. So conscious of these bureaucratic activities were the Mesopotamian literati, that they projected – as the Chinese did later – earthly bookkeeping into the nether world. Cuneiform texts refer to the scribe of the ruler of the dead who keeps lists with the names of all those who are to die each day. Linked with the reciprocity between ruler and ruled was the elaboration of concepts of justice and of a formal legal system in Mesopotamia as in Egypt – a legal system that increasingly regularized the duties and functions of scribes and administrators, while also expanding these functions.

In Egypt, in India, especially under the Mauryan Empire of 321–185 BC, in China and later in Central and South America and in many other parts of the world, much the same took place – great public works were undertaken, complex bureaucracies were established. Important to these administrative activities was the invention of systems of writing. They were based, in the first instance, on pictorial or logographical techniques for labelling the bags and jars of merchandise to indicate their content – oil, grain etc. These are now thought, in the Middle East, to go as far back as 8000 BC. Great ingenuity and elaboration were required to expand their scope as a system of representation for a growing range of activities, objects, purposes and even languages. The Mesopotamian scribe, expected to be bilingual in Sumerian and Akkadian, developed a script based on logos into an intricate cuneiform 'code' flexible enough to survive and deal with the shift from Sumerian to Tigro-Akkadian to Old Babylonian or Euphrato-Akkadian as well as the intrusion of such foreign languages as Hittite, Elamite, Hurrian and Urartian. All this was done without developing an alphabetic or fully and consistently phonetic mode of representation, though symbols were used both phonetically and ideogrammatically soon after 3000 BC. The richness and complexity of Chinese writing have long been well known and the specialized instruction and labour necessary for learning it have been well understood. The same applied, of course, to the Egyptian hieroglyphic and, perhaps, to the later systems of representation or of aiding the memory developed in Central and South America. Even in Sumer, consistent and rigorous instruction in writing – the training of scribes – began early.

The dozen or so cities that had constituted Sumerian civilization around 3000 BC were initially independent, ruled by councils composed of aristocratic elders. They developed law, administration and the use of money. Before the emergence of kingship, they saw their cities and temples as economies administered by and for a chief god, helped by dependent lesser gods having functional roles. The mythological hierarchy of God–administrators and divine servants, preserved for the main temple of the city of Lagash, for instance, no doubt reflects the earthly administrative hierarchy that actually performed the organizing and supervising work in the temple economy. At the apex of the human hierarchy stood the *ensi* or manager, expected to administer and uphold the functions of the estate and to carry out the commands of the owner – the god – who spoke through signs and omens. The Sumerian cities, around 3000 BC, contained several thousand inhabitants each and elected a single leader, the *lugal* (literally 'the big man') as military commander in time of war. He served for a limited period and returned to his normal occupation when the emergency had ended. Five centuries later, the population of all Sumer exceeded half a million and four-fifths of its people probably lived in cities. Uruk, the first of the developed city-states, housed nearly 50,000 people and surrounded itself with a wall 10 kilometres long, though it also controlled seventy-six outlying villages. As war became more and more frequent, the *lugal* became king, extending his period of rule.

The incessant warfare between city-states in the third millennium BC strengthened and centralized internal organization and control in those states and expanded the role of government, as well as the number of slaves. But there was also internal tension within states. A Sumerian tablet describes reforms undertaken in the city-state of Lagash around the year 2350 BC by King Urukagina, righting the worst abuses of the previous regime – high taxes, oppressive laws and corrupt officials. Those exactions, the tablet states, were imposed in wartime and improperly continued into peace. Within a few years, however, the foreign king Sargon of Akkad was uniting the Sumerian city-states into the first Mesopotamian Empire. Its fall around 2150 BC was presaged by a series of rebellions in the subject states. It was followed by a period of decentralization in southern Mesopotamia until the third dynasty of Ur, between 2100 BC and 2000 BC, re-established regional hegemony. That dynasty set up a vast bureaucracy to collect taxes and tribute, expanded the system of irrigation and flood control and presided over a significant growth of population and settlement.

The Sumerian city-states belonged to a single culture, which admitted innumerable city gods and functional deities to its pantheon. But their incessant warfare prevented any dynasty from lasting and Sumeria from becoming a great political empire. It came frequently under the control of other people, the Elamites, the Semitic nomads of Akkad and then the Guti – all of whom learnt from those they conquered. After 2000 BC power shifted to the Amorite kings in the north, who built their capital in Babylon. Here Hammurabi, as king, proclaimed his famous laws, centralizing legal authority and replacing temple managers by secularized royal officials and a paid public service. Basically,

Sumerian culture and religion were adopted with few changes by the Amorites, and the Kassites, Assyrians and Chaldeans who followed. Between the ninth and the seventh centuries BC, a resurgent Assyrian polity held a vast empire and much of the Near East by military force and vigorous centralized control from the king's business office until defeated by the Medes in 614 BC. A once more briefly resurgent Babylon was then conquered by Cyrus the Great. Mesopotamia was incorporated into a succession of Near Eastern empires – Achaemenid, Seleucid, Parthian, Sassanian and Islamic. Darius, seizing the Achaemenid Empire in 522 soon after the death of Cyrus the Great and vastly extending it by conquests in India, Thrace and Macedonia, aimed to establish a firmly controlled and administered but contented state. He divided the Empire into twenty satrapies, each governed by a trusted official, usually a Persian, from the king's home state of Iran. He created a carefully supervised network of roads to facilitate administration, imposed a new system of land tax, planned a canal through the Isthmus of Suez and built prodigiously, especially at Susa and Persepolis. He standardized weights and measures, transferred populations, imposed control on frontier nomads and promulgated a legal code almost certainly based on that which Hammurabi had proclaimed in early Babylon and which in turn drew on earlier Mesopotamian codes. For the student of imperial bureaucracies, but for the student of the transience of power as well, the dams and irrigation systems of the Tigris and the Euphrates prove very fertile ground indeed. It was from the Persian (Achaemenid) Empire that the Greeks and their students derived the concept of the Near Eastern despot who was absolute lord of land and water in his kingdom and who dominated his subjects, from the highest to the lowest, in the same way.

The growth of bureaucracy: Egypt

The first more stable, consistent and highly elaborate bureaucratic administration known to us in some detail is that which governed ancient Egypt. The Egyptian myth of the state was profoundly religious, however, with scribes paying little if any attention, in their historical records, to social and economic matters as such. That state, from the beginning of recorded history in Egypt with the Old Kingdom of 3000–2150 BC, was centred on the person of the pharaoh – the ruler who guaranteed and maintained both the cosmic order and its earthly counterpart, law and order in society. The two kinds of order were aspects of the same thing to the Egyptian mind and were called *ma'at*. The pharaoh's rule had to be and according to the texts always was in accordance with *ma'at*. He was its earthly representative (through his contact with the gods), its carrier and its servant. His title 'pharaoh' meant 'great house' – the ruler was so sacred that his personal name was not to be mentioned. In the first three dynasties of the Old Kingdom he was said to be Horus, the falcon god who with his outstretched wings protects the country and whose fierce eyes are the sun and moon. The pharaoh was the reincarnation of a sacred power, the personification of an institution of divine origin. Until recently, he has been presented in modern Western literature as the archetypal god–king. Now, students of Ancient Egypt place greater emphasis on the ability of the ancient Egyptians to indulge in complementary ways of thinking, to conceive of kingship as human and divine at the same time. The king was a god in his capacity of king but he had not all the powers of gods – he was not miracle-working, he did not heal the sick, he did not bring rain. His earthly rule, his maintenance of order in his realm, was through earthly means.

Serious Egyptologists put much emphasis on the paucity and obscurity of contemporary and even later records of the Old Kingdom, on how little we know. It is still a matter of controversy whether the emergence of an Egyptian state and royal administration in 3000 BC was an autochthonous event or a direct result of Sumerian influence or example. Later Egyptian historians and the state myth in Egypt linked the formation of the state specifically with the unification of the Two Lands (Upper and Lower Egypt). This supposedly originated with the conquests of Menes, a King of Upper Egypt, who was said to have founded the capital Memphis at the point where the lands adjoin each other. (Modern research suggests that the unification of the two territories was a slow process beginning before the first historically attested dynasty. The dualism of Upper and Lower Egypt persisted for millennia and was reflected in royal titles and the form of the administration. Whether there was an actual war in which the two parts became unified is quite uncertain.)

Others, already early in the twentieth century, traced the unity and the specific form of the Egyptian government to the demands of irrigation (according to Wittfogel, primarily flood control) and its administration. The yearly inundation by the Nile, it was said, resulted in an agriculture that required irrigation and flood control, a complicated system of canals and ditches, dykes and dams, sluices and basins. The construction of these and the regulation of water supplies to farmers required a strong centralized government which learnt, in the process, to organize large bodies of workmen and to erect such monumental public works as the pyramids, which also date back to the middle of the Old Kingdom, around 2600 BC. The argument sounds reasonable and we know that records of the level of the Nile were kept systematically already in the Old Kingdom. But we have absolutely no knowledge of the actual irrigation system at the time of the Old Kingdom and some have argued that it emerged only at the time of the Middle Kingdom, being preceded by the construction of pyramids for purely religious motives. Even for the New Kingdom (1550–1080 BC) data are scarce. Max Weber believed, as Karl Wittfogel did, that the overriding importance in Egypt of systematic centralized river regulation and the huge construction projects that characterized Egyptian civilization produced a state based on compulsory labour – even though private property was also strong. 'As early as the Old Kingdom the entire people was pressed into a hierarchy of clientage, within which a man without a master was considered a good prize and, if apprehended, simply assigned to the pharaoh's draft labor gangs.'[8]

It is generally agreed, and confirmed by the surviving inscriptions with their large number of titles, that the Egyptian state bureaucracy emerged out of the royal household. Initially it ruled with very limited personnel, assisted by the royal princes and their private servants. In the early period, high officials were the sons, brothers, uncles, and nephews and cousins of the king. Among the oldest of the high offices was that of 'seal keeper of the king' – the man who was in control of the pharaoh's income in kind (Ancient Egypt used no money) and of the storerooms

8 Weber, op. cit., p. 1044.

and workshops of the royal residence. Another official – 'master of the largesses' – was responsible for the redistribution of food and other commodities among members of the royal household and royal servants in the widest sense. Taxes were paid in kind, assembled in the storerooms of the royal residence and later redistributed, in some instances after being converted into garments, to a relatively large portion of the population. The temples appear to have played a special part in this system.

Lower level state offices developed out of the private service of king and palace. As Jac J. Janssen notes in an article from which I have drawn much other information,[9] the later 'departments' in the state organization were indicated by a word which may originally have meant room (in the palace). In Egypt, by the end of the Old Kingdom, as in other societies, words for personal servants – such as the king's hairdresser – appear to have become honorific titles suggesting councillor or confidante. Whether they were attached to specific functions in the state administration is not always certain; some certainly were. By the third dynasty, the first stage of a permanent bureaucracy, ruling to some extent in its own right, had developed; the treasury became independent of the royal palace and was permanently located in Memphis. A supreme office of vizier was created – charged with general administration of the country in its entirety on behalf of the pharaoh, controlling the economy, law and the provincial administration. By the fifth dynasty, we find only commoners as viziers. All state officials, however, were scribes – whose work had been made much more convenient by the invention of papyrus and the continued innovative reworking of the script. They were trained in writing and in the art of drawing up decrees and other documents. By the second half of the period of the Old Kingdom, the forms of decrees had become so fixed as to suggest regularized bureaucratic practice of fairly long standing.

The position of temples and priests in this system is both important and unclear. Since the pharaoh was and remained the high priest of every temple, priests probably had little if any independent political power. It has been suggested that some priestly functions evolved from functions in the palace household and that lower officials acted as priests of the guardian divinities

9 Jac J. Janssen, 'The Early State in Ancient Egypt', in Claessen and Skalník, op. cit., pp. 213–34.

of their specific departments. Max Weber, however, stressed that the temples acquired economic immunities early and were granted immense properties by the Ramessides in the New Kingdom. Temple retainers and officials had been freed from compulsory services long before, in the third millennium BC. By the time of the New Kingdom, the priests and the royal officials had become the major privileged strata confronting the masses, in control of *corvée* labour and taxation and, on behalf of the pharaoh, of royal enterprises and trade monopolies, the domestic production of unfree labour and the agricultural output of the *coloni*. From the dawn of the historical period at the beginning of the third millenium BC, the Egyptian administration had recorded the annual level of the Nile flood and conducted a regular census of the population. From the second dynasty onward there was a diennial census of gold and fields. The state, from an early period, guaranteed private property and the execution of deeds of conveyance by registering them. Formal contractual agreements, administration of estates, syndicates and endowments were widespread. Private property, however, was strong in Egypt and there were periods when the religious cult of royalty weakened and even disorganized the administrative system, while the wealth given to the temples impoverished the crown. When administrative functions themselves were handed over to privileged servants of the court, when taxes were farmed out, provincial governors arrogated the rights of royalty and a period of 'feudalism' emerged. These trends were strongest during the interregna that separated the Kingdoms, and sometimes individual dynasties, from one another.

Egyptian administration, like that of Sumer and the Near Eastern empires, varied from period to period in its specific details. But the Egyptian state was politically continuous for a much longer period than any of the Near Eastern empires and it was held together, at least officially, much more strongly by the person of the ruler from the beginning. In practice, however, the early division of the Kingdom into administrative districts or *nomes* under a *nomarch* appointed by the pharaoh led more readily to fragmentation. It was in the *nomes* that irrigation and production and practical tax collection were carried out. The *nomarch* was responsible for royal administration in his area and for the community generally, but he also controlled the local militia. He officiated as district judge and as clerk of works for the temples and other public structures in his area. He was assisted by two royal deputies, who were the king's spies, but it was the *nomarch* who employed a large staff of officials – scribes, technicians and workers – and who was the day-to-day ruler of his province. As Egypt's conquests grew, whole countries were cared for by viceroys directly appointed by the pharaoh.

Students of public administration are inclined to see the Egyptian system as forming a series of public administrative services rather than a single centralized bureaucracy in the organizational sense. E.N. Gladden[10] lists various spheres of public administration:

1 The royal court and household, involving estate management, supply services and ceremonial organization.
2 The nation's productive machine which, while depending largely upon individual agriculturalists, called for extensive state planning in the sphere of hydraulic engineering.
3 Service of the cult of the dead, eventually developing into a colossal programme of pyramid building and other construction work.
4 The local government areas, closely affected by (2) and involving a wide delegation of executive powers.
5 The conduct of foreign relations, ranging from the normal practices of diplomacy to the imposition of imperial rule.

From the early tombs, we learn of such officials as Superintendent of the Inundation and Royal Constructor; in the sixth dynasty, a high official, trained as a steward, held in turn the post of judge general, master of works and hydraulic engineer. The founder of the nineteenth dynasty, a great general, served his initial apprenticeship as a royal scribe.

That the power of the centre declined in the second half of the Old Kingdom for a significant period is not in doubt; the causes are. The pharaoh himself in the course of the fourth dynasty began to be conceived as the son of the sun–god Re rather than as Horus, protector of the country. The independence of officials and the extent of private property increased and an economically

10   E.N. Gladden, *A History of Public Administration*, vol. I: *From Earliest Times to the Eleventh Century*, London, 1972, p. 53.

independent class of functionaries, sustained by estates attached to a given office that tended to become hereditary, emerged. The institution of *nomes* facilitated this development. The pharaohs reacted by instituting a central office to oversee these regions and their governors. With new dynasties and new kingdoms, central authority was restored, lost or weakened and restored again – but over the long term bureaucratic administration and arrangement expanded and developed strongly enough to be adopted by a series of invaders, from the Hyksos, through the Assyrians to the Persians and the troops of Alexander the Great. The tension between consistent and coherent rule-bound bureaucratic administration and what Weber calls patrimonial administration in which bureaucratic positions and functions were treated as property by those who exercised them remained a central theme – in this, as in other, ancient bureaucracies. S.N. Eisenstadt, who connects many of these features with the political systems and requirements of empires, has followed Edward Shils in stressing the importance and internal logic of centre–periphery relations in later imperial and imperial feudal societies, where central authority also rests to an important extent on a cultural and social tradition that reconstructed and evaluated social reality and the cosmic and socio-political order, and provided symbols of collective identity as well as the major modes of legitimacy. The major characteristics of such centre–periphery relations, Eisenstadt writes,

were a high level of distinctiveness of their centres; the perception of the centre as a distinct symbolic and organizational unit, and sustained attempts by the centres not only to extract resource from the periphery but also to permeate and reconstruct it according to the centre's premises. The political, and to some degree, cultural-religious centres in these societies were conceived as autonomous foci of the charismatic elements of the socio-political, and often also of the cosmic-cultural order. These centres – political, religious and cultural – were the foci and loci of the various great traditions that developed in these societies, distinct from local traditions not only in content but also in the symbolic and organizational structural characteristics. The permeation of the periphery by the centres was discernible in the development of widespread channels of communication which emphasized their symbolic and structural difference, and in the attempts of these centres, even if only to a limited degree, to break through the ascriptive ties of the groups at the periphery.

Closely connected to such centre–periphery relations is strong articulation – especially among the higher strata – of symbols of social hierarchies and stratification, of countrywide strata-consciousness and of tendencies to some political articulation and the expression of such consciousness, as well as a high degree of ideological symbolization and mutual orientations among the major religious, political and even ethnic and national communities. Although such communities tended to attain a relatively high degree of autonomy as well as distinct boundaries, yet in most of these civilizations, they also tended to constitute mutual referents of each other.[11]

China and its literati

To modern men and women, no ancient society has seemed so thoroughly, so sophisticatedly and so successfully bureaucratized over millennia as the Chinese. To the enlightened thinkers and despots of seventeenth- and eighteenth-century Europe – to which China almost certainly introduced the idea of *written examinations* and where it subsequently strengthened the concept of a civil service – China seemed the model of a philosophically governed society, elevating through its scholar-officials, the literati, moral probity and rational knowledge in the conduct of social affairs. To the *laissez-faire* thinkers of the nineteenth century, with their promotion of private property and individual enterprise against oppressive and backward-looking states concerned with preventing change, China became, on the contrary, the model of a static, unenterprising oriental despotism in which the weight and self-interest of a bureaucratic governing class inhibited economic development and social progress. It was seen, falsely, as the society of the eternal standstill – a grim warning, in the eyes of later generations, of the stultification linked with bureaucratic control. The existence in China, since ancient or relatively ancient times, of an elaborate and highly

11 S.N. Eisenstadt, 'Comparative Analysis in State Formation in Historical Contexts', *International Social Science Journal*, vol. XXXII, 1980, pp. 624–54 at p. 626. See also Edward Shils, 'The Concept of Consensus', in *International Encyclopedia of the Social Sciences*, New York, 1968, vol. 3, pp. 260–6, his *Center and Periphery: Essays in Macrosociology*, Chicago, 1975, and S.N. Eisenstadt, *The Political Systems of Empires*, New York, 1963, passim.

organized civil service, of great public works and of hundreds of thousands involved in *corvée* labour on great walls, mighty tombs and long canals, was and is not in dispute. Even more remarkable, and as central to the history of China, is the early emergence of a strong sense of Chinese culture or civilization, agriculturally based, kinship-dominated, at least among the nobility. This seems to have preceded political unity while making it possible for successive federations of tribes to inherit each other's traditions and claims. Even before the unification of the empire in 221 BC a new king laying waste the territory of a rival state left standing the ancestral tombs and symbols of the previous rulers in recognition of the 'universal' importance of the ancestor cult. By that time, Chinese historical writing had traced the origins of competing states and their ruling houses to acknowledged descent from and infeudation by the kings and culture-heroes of China's earliest dynasties – the Xia and the Shang-Yin – and even earlier legendary rulers.

China is the oldest continuous civilization and state in the world, though by no means the oldest state, empire or system of administration. It is, of early civilizations, the most elaborate, historically minded and self-conscious. For at least 3,000 years it has been systematically administered. The picture drawn by Etienne Balazs, though true of China only for the past 2,000 or 1,500 years, *is* the picture that Chinese themselves have drawn of their society for those two millennia, though it also owes much to Marx or, at least, coincides with his insights:

China was a large *agrarian* society, highly developed but using traditional techniques, and established on a sub-continent that lacks any marked geographical articulation. Its cells, scattered over an immense territory whose main arteries were a system of waterways, existed in an economic autarchy that made each of them an individual unit, and isolated each unit from every other. These cells were the peasant families that composed the overwhelming majority of the population. They were self-sufficient; but without the system of economic exchanges and the organizational framework imposed from above, they would have disintegrated irremediably into their component particles, into an anarchy that would have made impossible not only the distribution, but also the production of goods, and indeed the maintenance of life itself. It was, in other words, a pre-industrial, non-maritime society, based on a peasant subsistence economy.

This society was *bureaucratic* because the social pyramid – which rested on a broad peasant base, with intermediate strata consisting of a merchant class and an artisan class, both of them numerically small, lacking in autonomy, of inferior status, and regarded with scant respect – was capped and characterized by its apex: the mandarinate.

The class of *scholar-officials* (or mandarins), numerically infinite-simal but omnipotent by reason of their strength, influence, position, and prestige, held all the power and owned the largest amount of land. This class possessed every privilege, above all the privilege of reproducing itself, because of its monopoly of education. But the incomparable prestige enjoyed by the intel-ligentsia had nothing to do with such a risky and possibly ephemeral thing as the ownership of land; nor was it conferred by heredity, which after all can be interrupted; nor was it due solely to its exclusive enjoyment of the benefits of education. This unproductive elite drew its strength from the function it performed – the socially necessary, indeed indispensable, function of co-ordinating and supervising the productive labor of others so as to make the whole social organism work. All mediating and adminis-trative functions were carried out by the scholar-officials. They prepared the calendar, they organized transport and exchange, they supervised the construction of roads, canals, dikes, and dams; they were in charge of all public works, especially those aimed at forestalling droughts and floods; they built up reserves against famine, and encouraged every kind of irrigation project. Their social role was at one and the same time that of architect, engineer, teacher, administrator, and ruler. Yet these managers before their time were firmly against any form of specialization. There was only one profession they recognized: that of governing. A famous passage from Mencius [390–305 BC] on the difference between those who think and those who toil perfectly expresses the scholar-officials' outlook: 'Great men have their proper business, and little men have their proper business . . . Some labor with their minds, and some labor with their strength. Those who labor with their minds govern others; those who labor with their strength are governed by others. Those who are governed by others support them; those who govern others are supported by them'.

Being specialists in the handling of men and experts in the political art of governing, the *scholar-officials were the embodiment of the state*, which was created in their image – a hierarchical, authoritarian state, paternalistic yet tyrannical; a tentacular welfare state; a totalitarian Moloch of a state. The word 'totalitarian' has a modern ring to it, but it serves very well to describe the scholar-officials' state if it is understood to mean that *the state has complete control over all activities* of social life, absolute domination at all levels. The state in China was a managerial, an interventionist state – hence the enduring appeal of Taoism, which was opposed to state intervention. Nothing escaped official regimentation. Trade, mining, building, ritual, music, schools, in fact the whole of public life and a great deal of private life as well, were subjected to it. [12]

Balazs here dramatizes the spirit; the anomalous details are discussed in the rest of his book. Here he portrays a whole social system as flowing, inevitably, by logical necessity from what he presents, perhaps excessively, as an atomized peasant mass. Yet the result he postulates was there for all to see. Some traditional Chinese historiography to the contrary, it was not there from the beginnings of Chinese political society. It took time to evolve. The title emperor (*huang-di*) was not used by any historical ruler before the unification of the empire in the third century BC. Earlier rulers were at best overlords, receiving honours and tribute, reserving to themselves the sole right to perform the sacrifice to the Gods of the Earth and the Sky and the regal title Son of Heaven (*Tien-zi*). Their feudal lords and administrators were relatives and clan associates (including wives, who were granted fiefs and authority). The bureaucratized empire we know evolved out of the collapse of a dominantly feudal system, in parts of which administration and state power began to develop more independently. It evolved also out of a loose confederation of tribes and states, in which power could pass rapidly from one to the other and in which states were often at war. Yet a sense of belonging to the same culture and civilization and its aristocratic/ political ancestor cult seems to have been strong from the earliest times.

For two thousand years at least, the Chinese have systematically exaggerated their considerable antiquity as a civilization and projected to the dawn of history their empire and its systematically bureaucratic and agro-managerial foundations. The traditional mythical history, elaborated by scholars from the sixth century BC onward, went thus: After Heaven and Earth were separated and the world came into being, the universe was ruled by twelve

12 Etienne Balazs, *Chinese Civilization and Bureaucracy: Variations on a Theme*, transl. H.M. Wright, New Haven, Conn., 1964, pp. 15–17.

successive Emperors of Heaven, each of whom reigned for 18,000 years. They were succeeded by the eleven Emperors of the Earth, each reigning for a similar period, and then by the nine Emperors of Mankind, who reigned altogether for another 45,000 years. Throughout this period people were naturally virtuous; laws and punishments were not required. There followed sixteen sovereigns of whom we are given only their names, and then the three sovereigns: Fu-Xi, who tamed wild beasts for food and sacrifice and lived in Honan, south of the Yellow River; Shenung (the Divine Cultivator); and Huang-di, the Yellow Emperor (*huang*, 'yellow', has no connection with the *huang* in the title *huang-di*, emperor). The Yellow Emperor supposedly united the tribes into a great nation by defeating political rivals in war and was the first truly human ruler. He and his four successors – collectively the Five Sages – established the forms of government, the sacrifices to be made to the gods, the mountains and the streams, and the rules of morality and right conduct, including the principle of filial piety. Immediately after them, in the year 2205 BC (but according to the Bamboo Books, 1989 BC), their descendant Yu is said to have founded the first historical dynasty, the Xia, gaining pre-eminence by his great work – over thirty years – of regulating the floods by damming and altering the course of China's rivers and draining its marshes. His devotion to the task was so great, Confucius (551–479 BC) wrote that he did not enter his house for thirteen years, neglected his toilet and allowed his clothes to disintegrate.

Up to the foundation of the Xia we are clearly in the realm of mythology. For Yu and the other emperors of the Xia we have no contemporary evidence whatever, but from 1000 BC we do have references to the Xia as a historical dynasty existing from ancient times.

The first dynasty of which we have historical contemporary (archaeological) evidence is the Shang dynasty (circa 1766–1154 BC), which changed its name to Yin when it once more moved its capital half way through. The oracle bones and inscriptions left by this dynasty, when discovered less than 100 years ago, substantially confirmed the account of Shang kings given in the traditional writings, which date back to the fifth century BC. This has strengthened the probability that the seventeen rulers of the Xia dynasty, said to have reigned between 2183 and 1752 BC, were similarly historical. If we leave aside the ascription of generations of earthworks and irrigation labours to Emperor Yu himself, the historical account of the Xia dynasty is sparse and plausible, as is the average regnal period of twenty-five years, especially when contrasted with the 18,000 ascribed to mythical rulers. Traditionally, the Xia dynasty is credited with instituting land tax and tributes (both exacted in kind), with dividing its domains into nine administrative districts (one of which was a royal domain), with inventing the jade tablet as a symbol of authority or of its delegation and with establishing a judicial system.

The Shang–Yin dynasty saw the development of a bronze age culture in China, progress in architecture, metallurgy and trade, the rise of coinage and the institution of the well–field system for agriculture and taxation. Land in principle belonged to the state. Fields of 630 *mous* were divided into nine sections, the central section containing a well from which all fields could be irrigated, and a public farm. The outside eight sections were allocated to eight tillers who helped till the public farm in the centre in lieu of state tax. The central government of the Shang was composed of five departments with ministers to head them. These were education, justice, economic affairs, interior and defence. Succession in the ruling house was from older brother to younger brother, not, as later, from father to son. Villages, then as later, worshipped a variety of local nature gods; a national cult based on ancestor worship, worship of the Gods of Heaven and Earth and sacrifices for fertility, was in the hands of the nobility.

Like the Egyptians, the Chinese developed a conception of the ruler, the Son of Heaven, requiring and maintaining a universal harmony of earthly power and cosmic forces. His performance of the sacrifice at the beginning of the agricultural year was an event of major significance for the prosperity of the kingdom: it could not be performed successfully if the Son of Heaven was not morally pure. No one but the Son of Heaven could perform the sacrifices to Heaven and Earth. From this evolved the doctrine of the Mandate of Heaven: the belief that a ruler or dynasty would fall when their conduct no longer pleased Heaven. It is unclear whether this doctrine was current in time of the Shang–Yin or whether it was invented by the Zhou invaders who overthrew the Shang to legitimize their usurpation of the kingdom and of the title and role of Son of Heaven.

In the second half of the eleventh century BC, the last Shang–Yin king lost power to the tribal confederation of the Zhou, ethnic Chinese in contact with 'barbarians'. These invaded from the west (of China) and gave their name to the next dynasty, the first dynasty of which, from 841 BC, we have good historical records. Formally, that dynasty ruled until 256 BC, first as the Western Zhou and then from 771 BC, as the Eastern Zhou. In fact, though Chinese civilization and Chinese territory expanded throughout this period, China was not a unitary state. The period of the Eastern Zhou, covering the Spring and Autumn period, was dominated by the emergence, conflict and temporary pre-eminence of a whole series of states, over time some 110 of them. Fifty-two of these were liquidated; by the beginning of the period of the Warring States (453–222 BC) the remainder had been reduced to seven large and ten small states. In the next 200 years, the Seven Strongs absorbed the Ten Smalls and a new dynasty, the Qin (221–201 BC), unified China under a single emperor, the first to take the title *huang-di*. With that dynasty and its successors, the Former and Later Han dynasties that ruled from 206 BC to 220 AD, the Chinese empire and imperial administration became a unity, with Confucianism as its political ideology. (The Qin had been Legalists. They persecuted independent philosophical thought and Confucianism in particular in their struggle against traditional feudal authority and ideology.) Before that, we have a Chinese world of contending states and tribal federations, in which power is disturbed by the penetration, from the west, first of bronze and then of iron and in which kings (*wang*) or *hegemons* (*pa*) ruled specific territories with the support of clansmen forming an infeudated nobility. The power of dynastic rulers at that period, indeed, is derived from the pre-eminence of particular states. Yet, even then there appears to have been a looking backward to earlier dynasties and legitimation by real or pretended genealogical descent. The founders of the Zhou dynasty claimed, or were claimed by later scholars, to be descendants of a great statesman and feudal prince of Emperor Yu's time and – further back – of the Five (mythical?) Sages and thus of China's legendary first political ruler, the probably mythical Yellow Emperor, Huang-di. In Xia, Shang and Zhou times, the tradition has it, feudal princes in various parts of the nation and even far-flung frontier tribes called themselves the descendants of

Huang-di. And just as Chinese today call themselves the Han people – descendants of those who lived under the Han dynasty – so we find in Zhou times the expression *Ju-Xia* (all those descended from people who lived under the sway of the Xia) to signify the Chinese cultural domain, the 'we' as opposed to the 'they'.

The Chinese administrative system, supposedly, began in the Shang–Yin dynasty when the king of Shang divided land among his wives, sons and the nobility, installing them in feudal fiefs and dividing them into four ranks: *Hou* (Marquis). *Bei* or *Bo* (Earl), *Nan* (Baron) and *Tian*. The Zhou consolidated the rule of a paramount king, the Son of Heaven (*Tian-zi*), served by five ranks of feudal aristocrats: *Gong* (Duke), *Hou, Bo, Zi* (Viscount) and *Nan*. The Zhou, however, instituted an administrative class which included *Qing* (Minister), *Dafu* (Senior Officials) and *Shi* (Bachelors), who were the first professional officials in China. They were selected by recommendation (supplemented by examinations), granted land and often chosen on hereditary principles. They were neither historians and wizards as the officials of the Xia dynasty were reputed to have been nor simply aristocrats as Shang officials were supposed to have been. The importance of such professional officials was greatly strengthened by the institution, under the Zhou, of administrative districts, the *xian* (in the Giles–Wade transliteration, *hsien*), governed by such officials directly responsible to the central government. These officials were bureaucrats and not feudal administrators, a distinction neatly brought out by H.G. Creel[13] in making the point that the feudal lord can do in his fief whatever he is not forbidden to do, while the bureaucratic official may not properly do anything that is not part of his prescribed function. The *xian* system – a clear rival to feudal administration that ended by destroying it – had an earlier history in the State of Qin, a state especially active in the construction of irrigation works. Before its rulers became the Qin dynasty by conquering the whole of then 'China', the State itself had been totally divided into *xian* as early as 350 BC and there is evidence that the system existed even earlier in the neighbouring State of Yin, which had been divided into *xian* under administrative control by 543 BC. In the southern State of

13 H.G. Creel, 'The Beginnings of Bureaucracy in China: The Origins of the *Hsien*', *Journal of Asian Studies*, vol. XXII, 1964, pp. 155–83 at p. 164.

Qu, too, administration by officials was quite strongly developed by the seventh century BC and *xian* administrators were being moved about and used as functionaries a hundred years later. Creel, ascribing the origin of the *xian* system to the Qu, suggests that its elevation of state power over kinship is the result of barbarian influence – all the states in which the *xian* was developed were considered by contemporaries as Chinese but not properly so.[14] The system provided, in the end, an administrative solution to the conflicts and corruptions of feudal clans inherent in the then more traditional Chinese elevation of the ruler as senior representative of the ancestor and of feudal lord as sub-clan head. But it also made possible a very considerable extension of flood control and irrigation works.

Certainly, the Spring and Autumn period and even more the period of the Warring States saw a steady weakening of hereditary feudal positions and an expansion of the administrative apparatus controlled by the dukes of various states, who themselves became internally more powerful in the conflicts between states. In every principality, power was becoming more centralized. Hereditary feudal lords were being replaced by governmental officials directly dependent on the ruler. The process was consolidated by three institutions that spread through these principalities in the Warring States period: *zhilu zhidu* (the institution of emolument, by which officials were paid by the government, usually in grain and in accordance with their rank and duties), *xifu zhidu* (the institution of the seal, which officials held at the ruler's pleasure and with which they had to seal every order) and *shangzi zhidu* (the institution of budget and accounting). In the last, officials wrote down on wooden slips each year's budget in duplicate and sent one half to the king, who would receive the official's final report of revenue and expenditure at the end of the year and compare it with the forecast on the slip. Rewards and punishments for officials were determined on their performance in this respect.

With the unification of the empire, our picture of administration becomes still less speculative and better documented. The Qin dynasty abolished enfeoffment and divided the country into *jun* and *xian*, directly administered by centrally appointed officials, civil and military. A formal system of civil service

14   Ibid., pp. 171–82.

examinations was instituted by the Han (165 BC). In 124 BC, an imperial university was set up by the Emperor Han Wu-di in the Han capital Changan (now Xian) for the express purpose of inculcating in future officials the abilities, values and attitudes desired by the government. Similar training schools arose in the provinces – one in Sichuan is said to have preceded the imperial university. A modern Chinese scholar, Professor Zhang Jin-Jian, drawing on the carefully kept census figures, notes that the Han Empire at the peak of its population had 50,066,856 people (16,070,906 families) and 152,986 officials constituting 0.3 per cent of the total population. During the short-lived Xui dynasty in the sixth century AD (589–617 AD), there were 195,937 officials in a population of 46,019,966 (0.4 per cent of the total population). With the Tang Dynasty (established in 627 AD), the civil service expanded to 0.7 per cent of the population – 349,863 officials for just under 53 million people.

With the Han dynasty – after the Qin Emperor had repressed and ruined the old feudal nobility, already weakened by centuries of warfare – a new class, the *qunzi*, came fully into its own. Originally, the term had meant aristocrat. Confucius used it for the (morally) superior man, what Englishmen used to call a gentleman. With the elevation of a modified Confucianism to the state ideology of the Han empire, the *qunzi* became the educated man, reared in and ideologized by the Confucian classics, serving or ready to serve the state as an official. As early as the Han dynasty, Creel reminds us:

> the Chinese bureaucrat, far more than his counterpart in ancient Egypt, Rome or even Byzantium, depended for his professional advancement upon his evaluation by other officials on the basis of relatively objective criteria: grades obtained in examinations, experience in seniority, voluminous records of his performance in office, and merit ratings. The central government kept itself informed of local conditions by means of various systems of inspection and a voluminous flow of reports and statistics. It estimated its income and budgeted its expenditures . . . it sought to control economic activity and even at times to regulate prices.[15]

There are records, even, of officials measuring the girth of oxen while inspecting villages. At the time of the Northern Wei from 485 AD, China evolved a state distribution and control of

15 Ibid., pp. 156–7.

land that was applied more universally in the Sui and Tang. The system provided for the state to grant land to able-bodied males in specified allotments of two parts. The larger, intended for cereal crops, reverted to the state at death. The smaller, intended for mulberry orchards, could be retained in the family on a hereditary basis. In return, the holder was obliged to render labour service and to pay tax in kind. The system was intended, in the absence of universal use of money, to make tax collection and the distribution of products more effective, to reduce the landholdings and retainers attached to major landlords, to help reclamation of land and to spread out the population. The system became inoperable from 700 onward partly because the landholdings of officials and of Buddhist monasteries were retained in private hands and partly because administration of the system proved inefficient.

The basic outlines of the Chinese bureaucratic system established by the Qin and supplemented with examinations and special education by the Han remained those of Chinese administration for the next 2,000 years. Departments became more complex and grew in number, from three under the Western and Eastern Jin (265–420 AD), to six ministries and twenty-four branch departments under the Tang (618–906). Especially important was the Tang's development of the Censorate, divided into functional divisions. The first of these was concerned with general affairs, attended imperial audiences, and impeached officials for unjust and irregular actions. The second supervised affairs of the palace and ensured that proper procedures were followed. The third formed an inspectorate looking at the work, the efficiency and integrity of officials. Under the Song (Giles–Wade: Sung), in 1045 AD an additional section was added. Its task was to consider and criticize if necessary the policy of the most senior officials. By the time of the Ming (1368–1644) these six ministries or Boards – of personnel, of revenue, of rites, of war, of justice and of works – oversaw everything of significance in China. A system of recommendation, which made notables recommending an official co-responsible for his misdemeanours to one grade below the punishment meted out to the official, was devised – in elaborately systematized form – by the Song

16   On the Song bureaucracy see E.A. Kracke, *Civil Service in Early Sung China 960–1067*, Cambridge, Mass., 1953, and James T.C. Liu, *Reform in Sung China*, Cambridge, Mass., 1959.

Dynasty.[16] For much of the dynastic period China had a complex code of administrative or institutional law, setting out the functions of departments, duties of officials, etc. Its last imperial version, the eighteenth-century *Da Qing Hui Tien* was operative until (after) 1911.

In China, as in many other oriental societies, eunuchs appeared early as royal servants engaged in the daily service of the emperor. Their numbers appear to have grown from only thirty working in the palace during the Later Han to 3,000 under the Tang. Administratively, eunuchs belonged to a special department – the Department of Palace Service – later but not initially headed by a eunuch. By the Tang, there were five bureaux regulating the eunuchs, numbering seventy-two officials between them. From 780 AD, the royal army of the palace was commanded by eunuchs and their relatives. These came to play an important role in the succession of emperors. Their power dwindled under the Song and was strictly though not always successfully limited thereafter. In struggles between competing groups of officials, royal kinsmen and women and the emperor, eunuchs could at times play a significant role. But they were forbidden to rise above the third degree in rank. They were treated as physically and therefore morally deformed in Confucian ideology and the history of China in each dynasty was written by their enemies. However, eunuchs did become palace confidential secretaries and as such they could exercise important influence in communications between the emperor and his officials. There were also some eunuchs – the great Ming Admiral Zheng He (Cheng Ho) and the Qing General Cai Lun – who earned admiration for their achievements in war and exploration.

Professor Hans Bielenstein has studied the Han bureaucracy for us in careful detail (*The Bureaucracy of Han Times*, Cambridge, 1980) and we have some similar studies for later dynastic periods. All Han officials, whether belonging to the central administration or to local ones, were assigned to a position on a scale of eighteen ranks according to the remuneration that went with the official's current office, not with his seniority. The scale must originally have expressed the salary in kind which was due to the office-holder. Sixteen of the ranks are graded according to the number of *shih* that go with the post. (The term *shih* is an ancient measure of capacity, analogous to our bushel.) The scale, however, ceased to determine salaries directly and became simply a tool for ranking officials and posts on an abstract scale and determining privileges and protocol. Salaries continued to be fixed in relation to the scale in the sense that they increased with each higher step; they did not necessarily do so proportionally. The Former Han History (*Han shu*) and the Later Han History (*Hou Han shu*) give valuable descriptions and chronological tables of high officials; the Later Han History includes a more detailed Treatise on Bureaucracy. These texts, compiled in the first century AD and in the fifth century AD, are further supplemented by valuable second- and third-century AD commentaries. The Treatise on Bureaucracy in the Later Han History Professor Bielenstein dates on internal evidence as a contemporary document written between September 141 AD and September 142 AD.

The highest official in the early Han empire – above the scale of eighteen ranks and apparently not regularly appointed – was the Grand Tutor, notionally, though not always practically, responsible for the moral guidance of the emperor. Below him were the Three Excellencies: the Military Grand Commandant, the Chancellor and the Grandee Secretary. The Chancellor was in charge of the state budget, keeping financial accounts, maps, population and land registers and a roster of officials, grading their performance and recommending candidates for vacancies. The Grandee Secretary, whose duties are not made clear in the contemporary texts, ranked below the Chancellor and may at first have been his Chief Assistant. Chinese scholars have concluded from varied documentary evidence that the Grandee Secretary had responsibility for the judiciary supervision of all officials, acting like a modern procurator to prevent abuse of authority among officials of all ranks, in the imperial palace, the central government or the local administration. The Three Excellencies stood at the top of the scale of ranks, at some 10,000 *shih*. Their assistants came next, occupying places in the next four ranks of 2,000+*shih*, exactly 2,000 *shih* and 1,000+ *shih*. From here on, there are twelve more ranks going through 1,000 *shih*, 600 *shih*, 300 *shih*, 200 *shih* and 100 *shih* and two ranks of a more minor nature whose salaries are not expressed in *shih*. Additional ranks of 800 *shih* and 'equivalent to' 800 *shih* (two separate ranks) and 500 and the 'equivalent of' 500 *shih* existed until 23 BC but were abolished during that year. We do not know the meaning of the phrase that says literally 'equivalent of', but it marked a rank separate from the pay scale it was equivalent to.

The office staff of the Chancellor contained such officials as a Director of Uprightness, reporting illegal acts committed by officials (equivalent to 2,000 *shih*), two Chief Clerks ranking at 1,000 *shih*, a Master of Records and a Consultant (equivalent to 600 *shih*) and a Prefect of the Conscripts at the Gates, who protected the entrances to the Ministry.

The office staff of the Chancellor was organized into Bureaux of the East, of the West, of Memorials, of Gathering (Accounts) and of Consultation (giving advice). Division heads of these Bureaux ranked at 400 *shih*, Junior Division Heads at 300 *shih*, Associates at 200 *shih* and Foreman Clerk at 100 *shih*. During the course of the Former Han the Bureaux had increased from fifteen officials in the Bureaux of the East and the West to 382 in the whole Ministry by 117 BC.

The office of the Grandee Secretary was similarly organized with two Assistants (1,000 *shih*) and a Master of Records. One of the Assistants, who had his office in the palace precinct, was in charge of charts, registers and imperial books and the behaviour of palace officials. He passed on to the throne memorials from the Three Excellencies, the Ministers and the local administration and transmitted imperial edicts addressed to the commanderies and kingdoms.

The Palace Assistant Secretary, part of whose functions were later appropriated by Masters of Writing, was assisted by fifteen attending Secretaries who were probably organized into Bureaux, staffed with Junior Division Heads, Associates and Foreman Clerks. The latter, also known as Foreman Clerks of Clerkly Writing, were required to pass a test on their knowledge of 9,000 characters and all major styles of writing, which was administered by the Prefect Grand Astrologer.

The Grand Commandant, in charge of military affairs, later called Commandant-in-Chief, must have had subordinates probably organized in similar ways but the early texts say nothing about them. Generally, the military section of the bureaucracy became politicized early and the Commandant-in-Chief after 8 BC was reduced to being an ordinary member of the Cabinet. At that time the position of Grandee Secretary was abolished and replaced by that of the Grand Minister of Works, and ranked, with the Commander-in-Chief, at the same salary level as the Chancellor. The Three Excellencies now ranked at 10,000 *shih*. Within the scale there were now nine Ministers. Three of these, the Grand Master of Ceremonies, Superintendent of the Imperial Household and the Commandant of the Guards belonged to the Division of the Grand Commandant. The next three, the Grand Coachman, the Commandant of Justice and the Grand Herald belonged to the Division of the Grand Minister Over the Masses (the new title for the Chancellor). The remaining three, Director of the Imperial Clan, Grand Minister of Agriculture and Privy Treasurer, belonged to the Division of the Minister of Works, who had replaced the Grandee Secretary. The number of Bureaux in the various Ministries increased; so did the number of officials and their functions. These included not only administering sacred places, but preparing and arranging food for national sacrifices (the Prefect Grand Butcher), arranging ritual and court music, supervising the building of an ancestral temple at imperial grave mounds, organizing and performing divination (the Prefect Grand Augur and his Assistant), drawing up the calendar (the Prefect Grand Astrologer), overseeing the Academy for training officials and its educational standards, examining candidates, organizing prayers (the Prefect Grand Supplicator) etc. There were Gentlemen-in-Attendance-Rapid-as-Tigers (400 *shih*), Gentlemen-of-the-Palace-Rapid-as-Tigers (300 *shih*) and Rapid-as-Tigers-who-Attend-with-Integrity (200 *shih*). There were Gentlemen-of-the-Feathered-Forest and Cavalry-of-the-Feathered-Forest; there were Imperial Equipages and their Commandants in Attendance; there was Cavalry and Attendant Cavalry. There were Guards, Emergency Cohorts and Garrisons, all most carefully and systematically organized. There was a Prefect of the Stables of Fine Horses of the Left and a Prefect of the Stables of Fine Horses of the Right, each with their grooms. There was a Commandant of Justice as chief interpreter of the law with inspectors, referees and clerks. In the capital Changan there were twenty-six prisons for officials, each under a Prefect. The Empress had her own staff for her own palace, separate from the private apartments of the Emperor. The ladies of the harem were, characteristically, also organized into six ranks related to other bureaucratic ranks in the service of the state: Beautiful

Lady, Sweet Lady, 8th Rank Lady, 7th Rank Lady, Senior Maid and Junior Maid. The Emperor Wu (r. 140–87 BC) added the four ranks of Favourite Beauty, Graceful Lady, Elegant Lady and Compliant Lady. Emperor Yuan (r. 48–33 BC) added that of Brilliant Companion, who had a status equal to the Chancellor's. The Favourite Beauty ranked above the Nine Ministers. The Elegant Lady ranked at 2,000 *shih*, the Compliant Lady at 1,000+ *shih*, the Maid for All Purposes at 300 *shih* and the Tender Maid, the Pleasing Maid and the Soothing Maid at 100 *shih*. The harem ladies increased to 3,000 in number in the course of the Former Han. The founder of the Later Han did away with the bureaucratic ranking of the harem Ladies and used only three designations: Honourable Ladies, who received a fixed though small salary, and Beautiful Ladies and Chosen Ladies who were only granted gifts. The lowest of these groups – the Chosen Ladies – was the largest. By 166 AD its number had reached 5,000.

The staff of the Heir Apparent who, like the Empress, received a private income from forty prefectures, was organized on the same principles. So, for practical purposes, was everything else: architects, supervision of waters and parks, side gates and dependent states, the building of roads and canals, the officials associated with capital cities and their territories, provincial states and local administration. The titles of offices, the division of responsibilities, changed but by 5 BC there were 130,285 officials, systematically organized, examined, inspected – not just by one Excellency, but by three, by their staffs and their provincial inspectors.

If systematic Chinese administration is old and impressive, Chinese writing and discussion on administration is even older and just as impressive. The *Book of History* elaborated, well before the unification of the empire, the 'Great Plan', which dealt *inter alia* with the practice of the five businesses, earnest devotion to the eight objects of government, harmonious use of the five time arrangements and thoughtful use of the various verifications, the establishment and use of sovereignty, the correct use of the three virtues and the hortatory use of the five happinesses, and the deterrent use of the six extremities. The eight objects are government and food, commodities, sacrifices, provision of work, provision of education, punishment of crime, guests and the army. The three virtues are straightforward government, strong government and mild government, to be exercised according to the circumstances of the time. Usurpation of power by officials must be resisted by the ruler. As early as 330 BC, the political philosopher Shen Pu-hai, a highly successful chancellor of the small north-central state of Han (not to be confused with the Han dynasty), formulated principles of administration that became widely influential in Qin and Han times and were still cited in eighteenth- and nineteenth-century China. These are known – and have been collected by H.G. Creel – through quotations from a book doubtfully attributed to Shen himself but almost certainly substantially derived from his sayings. Shen Pu-hai, as Creel puts it,

> is concerned, with almost mathematical rigour, to describe the way in which a ruler can maintain his position and cause his state to prosper by means of administrative techniques and applied psychology ... He points out that it is utterly impossible for a ruler personally to know and deal with all of the particular aspects of his domain; he must make particulars manageable by grouping them in classes, and dealing with them as categories. Similarly he must allow no one minister to gain predominant power, but 'cause all of his ministers to go forward together, like the spokes of a wheel'. And he must deal with everything and every person by means of completely impersonal technique, with utter objectivity.[17]

Shen Pu-hai was a legalist, arguing – against Confucian thought – for the primacy of law, government and depersonalized rules and principles over custom, tradition and received morality. He was a very successful chancellor in his own state of Han. The state, surrounded by enemies, not firmly consolidated within, was one in which religious, traditional and even familial sanctions may have been weak. Shen Pu-hai places no reliance on them. Neither, however, does he elevate fear – as other legalists did; he emphasizes, rather, the affection the ruler will gain by devoting himself to the promotion of the common good through proper control and administration.[18] The book attributed to him was extant and cited as late as the seventeenth century, when the full text appears to have been irretrievably lost. It has been partly reconstructed from quotations by Creel, who emphasizes Shen's

17 Creel, op. cit., pp. 160–1.
18 See also H.G. Creel, 'The Fa-chia: "Legalists" or "Administrators"?', in *Studies presented to Tung Tso-pin on his Sixty-fifth Birthday*, Taipei, 1961.

rationalism in the Weberian sense and quotes him as writing: 'The intelligent ruler is like the trunk, the minister is like an arm ... The ruler controls the principles, the minister carries them out in detail. The ruler holds the controls, the minister carries on routine functions.'[19] Shen lays great stress on the orderly, hierarchical organization of all officials, on the careful allocation of titles and of duties in conformity with them, on the dangers of impromptu and informal decisions and on the demoralization that results from allowing a single minister to monopolize the confidence of the ruler.

The *Zhou Li*, probably composed in the fourth or third century BC, outlines an idealized version of the Zhou system of administration, while other authors attributed to early, probably legendary kings ruling around 2000 BC an elaborate system of ministers with specialized functions – supervision of agriculture, schools, forests, communications, public works, law, music and rites. Soon after the unification of the Empire, the author of another text, *The String of Pearls on the Spring and Autumn Annals*, is said to have provided the bureaucratic practices and procedures, the theoretical foundations of administration, adopted by the Han. Both policy and administrative law or procedure were discussed by scholars called together for the purpose. Such meetings were recorded as taking place in 51 BC and in 79 AD. Even more important, perhaps, were the twenty-six Standard Histories which covered the period of every Chinese dynasty from the unification of the Empire under the Qin to its fall in 1911. (The final dynastic history, that of the Qing or Manchu, was completed and published in Taipei in 1961.) These histories were written by scholar–officials for scholar–officials with the conscious aim of providing information and precedents, in detail, to equip officials and rulers as fully as possible in the art of government. An office of historiographers was maintained under each dynasty to help prepare the history of the previous dynasty and to collect and preserve reports and documents, to build up archives for the next.

The Empire of the Mauryas

The Indus Valley civilization that flourished between 2150 and 1750 BC, with great cities in the Punjab and Sind and more than

19 H.G. Creel, *The Origins of Statecraft in China*, vol. 1, Chicago, 1970, p. 443.

sixty other settlements, displayed remarkable cultural homogeneity over more than 1,000 miles. This suggests a high degree of centralization. There was intensive commercial contact with Mesopotamia and some 2,500 seals, inscribed with a pictographic script not yet deciphered, have survived. The language of the Indus Valley civilization and much else about it are not known. In the second half of the second millennium BC, Aryan tribes, related to the Iranians and Armenians, invaded from the west or northwest and merged with settler civilizations. Some 600 years later, King Bimbisara, the first important king of the north-eastern state of Magadha (now South Bihar), was reputed to have been the earliest Indian ruler to stress, in the second half of the sixth century BC, the need for administration as a basic part of his expansionist policies. His ministers were handpicked and their advice was followed. Subordinate officers were divided into various categories according to their functions; officials were appointed to measure land, evaluate crops and to see to the building of roads. Two hundred years later, the much more centralized and bureaucratized Mauryan Empire of 321–185 BC, founded by King Chandragupta, built on these foundations, on a steady expansion of the agricultural economy through the introduction of iron and the plough, on the weakening of the rival tribal states by the (impermanent) conquests of Alexander the Great and on the further spread of manufacture, urbanization and of monarchical states. In the Ganges Valley, the king, much earlier, had been merged with the state as ultimate owner of all land except that used for small-scale cultivation. Chandragupta thus collected land rent as well as a share of the produce, had animals assessed and taxed, placed commercial enterprises under government supervision and organized the large-scale transfer of *shudras* (cultivators) from overpopulated areas to newly cleared land. A new class of state helots emerged. King Chandragupta's mentor and advisor, Kautalya (fl. 321–296 BC), is often presented as the theorist of the new imperial system of taxation and administration. A treatise on government and economics, the *Arthasastra*, attributed to him (but its date is uncertain or, rather, in dispute, and its author may be a later figure also called Kautalya), refers at length to matters of taxation and related problems. Much of our picture of Maurya administration is drawn from it but confirmed by the Greek traveller Megasthenes.

The increasing power of the king – Chandragupta was said to be able to put into the field half a million men and 9,000 war elephants (almost certainly an exaggeration) – was accompanied by a similar increase in the power of the chief priest, whose religious calling fell into the background as he began to assume the functions of chief minister. (Kautalya, the king-maker who had installed Chandragupta, was a Brahmin.) Two key offices controlled by the central administration were those of Treasurer and Chief Collector. One was responsible for keeping account of the income in cash and for storing the income in kind; the other, assisted by a body of clerks, kept records of taxes. Separate departments of government had large staffs of superintendents and subordinate officers, local regional officers and central headquarters. The *Arthasastra* gives Machiavellian advice on ascertaining the character of ministers by temptation, winning over factions for one's own cause and against an enemy, keeping princes under restraint, using spies to detect disloyalty, corruption, embezzlement, wicked living and 'youth of criminal tendency', for sowing the seeds of dissension and enticing kings by secret contrivances. Beyond and behind this, there was high moral purpose – a saintly king must keep his organs of sense under control but he must recognize the importance of wealth since charity and desire depend on wealth for their realization. The text discusses the duties of the principal offices of state and the appropriate management and behaviour of dependents in the family, of slaves and labourers. It lists separate superintendents of gold and goldsmiths, of the storehouse, commerce, forest produce, the armoury, weights and measures, tools, weaving, agriculture, liquor, slaughterhouses, prostitutes, ships, cows, horses, elephants, chariots, infantry, passports and the city. Inns, hostels, serais (caravan inns) and places of entertainment were to be under strict surveillance and reports were to be received concerning strangers and frequenters. Cities were controlled by a mayor whose staff had the duty of keeping registers of persons and property. Villages were under a headman officially nominated. Even under the Maurya, however, as throughout subsequent Indian history, village autonomy under the headman prevailed at the base of civil administration. The village headmen consulted with the elders. The rights and duties of the village barber, washerman, potter and blacksmith and responsibility for proper cultivation were decided on the basis of custom. Above the village headmen stood superiors in charge of five or ten villages and, above them, officials ruling large areas, attended by executive, revenue and police officials. In the edicts of Asoka, grandson of Chandragupta, the highest local officials, set over hundreds of thousands of persons and reporting directly to the great ministers of state, were termed *rajukas*, a designation pointing to functions connected with surveys, land settlement and irrigation. A vast army of minor officials dealt not only with public works, but with the maintenance of families of slain soldiers and of officials dying in office, as well as with helpless persons. The business of the treasury, indeed, was minutely organized, at least in theory, with distinctions between current, recurrent, occasional and other expenditure and checks to be applied to all of them.

The salaries of officials and expenditure on public works were high, one-quarter of the total revenue being reserved for them. The chief minister and the army commander received 48,000 *panas* each, the treasurer and chief collector 24,000 *panas*, ministers 12,000 *panas*, accountants and clerks 5,000 *panas* and state-employed artisans 120 *panas*. (We know neither the value of the *pana* nor the intervals at which these salaries were paid, but the ratio of a clerk's salary to that of the most senior official comes out at 1:96 and the ratio of the artisan's to that of the minister as 1:100.) Public works included dams (one, built by a governor, functioned for 800 years), irrigation, building and maintaining roads, wells and resthouses, running mines and state manufactures and subsidizing religious institutions and individuals. Water for irrigation in some areas was distributed and measured by the state. Water tax was collected when the state helped in providing irrigation. An interesting and important aspect of Mauryan administration – it had also been emphasized and used earlier in Mesopotamia – was the regularized use of spies, working in disguise (in India as recluses, householders, merchants, ascetics, students, mendicant women and prostitutes) to report on the mood of the population, the activities and reputation of local officials, etc. There were also *episcopoi* mentioned by Diodorus, who were not spies in the strict sense but superintendents making secret reports to the king. In the time of Asoka, the administrative system was further expanded and perfected. Written orders and edicts were circulated and read to the public. Officials were required to tour the country at regular intervals of two to five years. A ministerial council was expected to communicate all administrative measures adopted by the king to lower officials. The council itself, though subject to the king's will, at times had considerable power in helping to determine that will.

Mauryan administration, nevertheless, though imposing strong central control, appears to have been a highly personalized form of administration. It elevated a network of personal relationships, ultimately based on the ruler and very dependent on his ability. This, together with the socio-economic unevenness of the Mauryan Empire, aggravated by its rapid expansion and a Brahmin revolt against the low-born Mauryans and their heterodox social ideology, probably accounts for the rapid decline of the Empire after Asoka's death and its fragmentation into regional kingdoms. India had not the strong sense of fundamental cultural and political unity derived from the elevation or invention of common ancestors that dominated China. Neither did the Maurya succeed in creating a depersonalized official corps, loyal to the institution as much as, if not more than, the person of the emperor, bound together by an ideology and a professional *esprit* which made it possible for the bureaucracy and its values and procedures to survive while dynasties fell apart or were even replaced by foreign conquerors.[20]

The Inca

The Inca were not, in the temporal sense, an ancient bureaucracy. A Quechua-speaking people of the Cuzco region of Peru, they subjugated the area between Ecuador and Chile and welded some four-and-a-half to seven-and-a-half million people into a centralized, highly organized empire in less than a century before the arrival of the Spaniards in 1532. Non-literate, they used knotted cords – the *quipus* – to record numerical information

20 For the account of Kautalya's India, I have drawn on the Pelican *History of India*, vol. 1, by Romila Thapar, London, 1966, especially pp. 55–6, 82–3; the *Cambridge History of India*, vol. 1: *Ancient India*, ed. E.J. Rapson, 2nd Indian repr., Delhi, 1962; and Sudarsan Seneviratne, 'The Mauryan State', in Claessen and Skalník, eds, *The Early State*, pp. 381–402. The Arthasastra itself is available in an English translation by R. Shamasastry, *Kautalya's Arthasastra*, Mysore, 1961.

and as a mnemonic device; ignorant of the wheel or of the smelting of iron, they probably did not have a recorded calendar. They had mastered the techniques of irrigation, terracing, crop fertilization and crop rotation as the foundation for a highly intensive agriculture producing maize, squash, beans, potatoes, many other vegetables and fruit. These they stored on a large scale by drying or freezing. Their principal domestic animal, the llama, carried burdens while providing wool and meat. There was extensive mining and sophisticated use of copper, silver, gold, tin, mercury and arsenic. There were large-scale buildings, temples, palaces and fortresses, made of stone; there were elaborate irrigation works, water-piping systems and canalization of rivers. The empire was linked by an extensive network of roads; the central government required the maintenance of a system of post runners to permit rapid communication over great distances. The Inca were preceded by other highly developed agrarian, irrigating and terracing societies in Central and South America; the specific Inca contribution lay in their capacity for ruthless and effective organization.

The term 'Inca' can encourage confusion: it can mean the supreme ruler, or emperor, the Inca caste or original conquering tribes that ruled with him, the Inca culture or the entire Inca Empire, composed of various peoples with differing traditions and local customs. The basic material techniques on which the Inca Empire relied had been known and used in the Central Andean area for about 1,000 years before the Spanish conquest – the important developments that made the Inca Empire possible were increases in population size, and consequently in the application of such techniques as irrigation, and in the economic surplus. The specific genius of the Inca lay in the social and political organization of what was a classical conquest state, imposing its will on conquered populations, welding them – by force and strict regulation – into a coherent society with strong central government, an imposed common language, a developed system of economic, political and military control backed by harsh, observed laws, and a national cult – the Sun cult – involving human sacrifice. Loyal settlers from original or honorary Inca communities were resettled, on a large scale, in more recently conquered provinces. They were forbidden on pain of torture the first time and death the second to leave their new homes. Even their assimilation was forbidden by law; citizens who altered their manner of dress could be punished by a hundred blows. The natives were obliged to help the newcomers for the first two years of settlement after having built their houses for them. Some such resettlements involved large reciprocal transfers of population under minute government control. Much of the Inca obsession with conquest and administering new territories stemmed, it seems, from the fact that each new emperor had to start afresh – each ruler, as he died, continued to command the land and resources he held in life, and to be served by his court and retinue.[21]

The impact of the sixteenth-century Spanish discovery of the Inca Empire on European thought was immense. Here, it soon seemed, was the classical Utopia achieving universal welfare by strong, rational government, forcing people to labour for the common good, controlling or eliminating the ultimate basis of social divisiveness – private interest and private property used for private gain. The frankly despotic 'Socialist Empire of the Incas' became a great model for some and a grim warning for others, its very 'arithmetization' of social control arousing both admiration and horror.

Central to the functioning of the Inca state was the most pervasive control of land, labour, trade and the life and movement of the population as a whole. A hierarchy of officials, with the Inca as supreme head, was arranged in a decimal ladder, with one official for every 100 taxpayers, a superior for every 1,000 (or ten officials), another for every 5,000, 10,000 etc. All land, early European observers believed, belonged to the Inca, at least ultimately; alternatively, he had complete ultimate control of the usufruct. Certainly, land was divided into three basic types – land worked for the Inca (the government), land worked for the Sun (the national religion) and land held and cultivated in common by village communities and worked for themselves. Community lands were divided annually among taxpayers in proportion to the size of their families, with provision to take account of those absent on labour or other service. The community worked – for his benefit – the land of such an absentee. Taxes, it is usually stated, were paid in labour – partly on Inca

21 Geoffrey Conrad and Arthur A. Demarest, *Religion and Empire: The Dynamics of Inca and Aztec Expansionism*, Cambridge, 1984.

and Sun land, partly on public projects or in army service when required. But there was also payment in produce. An elaborate census system (using only the *quipus*) kept tax and administrative structure in balance. Land was inalienable; officials were maintained out of government storehouses and by the produce and labour of the communities they administered, which had the duties of building their houses, tending their flocks, providing one servant per 100 taxpayers ruled.

Local aristocrats and rulers appear to have been integrated into the structure of officialdom serving the Inca as all-powerful ruler. Individual grantees could be and were rewarded with land by the Inca for outstanding services in civil engineering (bridges and roads are mentioned), in war or in the Inca's household; such land was passed to heirs to enjoy the usufruct, but could not be divided or alienated. Neither was the right to a share – allocated by the senior kinsman – extinguished by absence.

The communities – or rather the women and non-taxpaying sons – were also obliged to weave cloth for the Inca and the Sun (out of the flocks belonging to the Inca and the Sun, tended by the community) and for themselves out of the wool of community flocks. Further they had to provide girls (usually under eight) for selection as 'chosen women', to be reared in special houses run by an official, the *apopanaca*, ultimately to serve the Inca and his relatives, or in religious establishments, or to be chosen for sacrifice. (Males were also taken for sacrifice, but it is not clear how they were chosen.) In theory, some 5 per cent of the able-bodied men in a community were at any time occupied in labour service for the state.

Exempt from tax for life, it appears, were all persons of Inca blood, all administrative officials in the decimal hierarchy down to those administering 100 taxpayers, all religious functionaries connected with the Sun cult, and all women (though they were liable to weave tax cloth or to become 'chosen women'). More limited exemption included all more minor officials during their period of office, specialists and craftsmen (who were obliged to work in their specialties, however), men over fifty and unmarried men under twenty-five, and the ill and incapacitated. Tax labour was supported, while at work, by the employer.

The poor, early observers report, were supported out of Sun or Inca storehouses. In law, poverty made theft excusable and might even provide a basis for punishing the master responsible for the dependent thief's poverty instead of the thief.

The Inca governed from Cuzco, the capital city, which had a population of 100,000 taxpayers – but which was a temple complex and ceremonial centre ringed by small villages with their own fields, rather than an urban centre proper. The Inca and his four most senior administrators – each in charge of one-quarter of the Empire – formed the Supreme Council that supervised all imperial affairs, administrative, judicial and military. The decimalized hierarchy of officials below them was subject to inspection by officers and special delegates sent directly from Cuzco, some of these every three years, some every two years, some annually and some as the need arose. Reports made by annual inspectors and the sending out of judges with power to punish violations seemed to be closely linked. The Inca could and did intervene in the activities of provincial governors; higher officials could invade the offices of lower officials and perform duties normally within the lower jurisdiction. The imposition of punishment was hierarchically controlled, with lower officials having limited powers. The legal system was harsh, with frequent reliance on the death penalty. Disrespect toward administrators was severely punished, so was the failure of administrators to punish or report crimes or to obtain authority before imposing the death penalty. Fleeing a place of residence where a taxpayer had labour obligations was punishable by death. All journeys required permission and travelling without such permission merited severe punishment.

Thomas More's *Utopia* was written more than a decade before the Spanish conquest of Peru. No one will be surprised, after reading this account, that some scholars have wondered whether More could have come across some verbal account of the Inca state derived from an earlier, secret discovery, perhaps by the Portuguese. Be that as it may, Inca Peru has served some, like Karl A. Wittfogel, as the perfect model of a simple 'hydraulic' agro-managerial despotism, in which all power, all privilege and all rewards derive from the managerial functions of the state, in which private property has no political power and in which everyone is totally dependent on the ruler. The material foundation of all this, for Wittfogel, is the organization of public works and *corvée* labour necessary for irrigation, terracing, etc. Others, like

Sally Falk Moore,[22] emphasize the extent to which the Incas took over or incorporated earlier traditional social arrangements of a 'feudal' character to form a state that was basically for the benefit of a land-owning class or caste. Anxious to stress that the official class was not paid by the state so much as it maintained itself by 'feudal' exactions from the communities it governed, she nevertheless presents us with a society in which the extent of state control and of state directed *corvée* labour is at first sight far more striking than local power bases and hereditary privilege. Subsequently, another scholar has indeed questioned whether Inca central control was in fact all that strong outside Cuzco by the time the Spaniards arrived. He reports that the Inca incorporation of local notables into their administrative hierarchy as well as the increasing number of land grants as a personal reward for services undermined central control and that the Empire was near disintegration.[23]

To what extent, however, were these ancient societies truly bureaucratic societies? For each one of the states or empires considered, there have been serious scholars to question whether the 'true' ruling class in each society consisted of state-dependent bureaucrats or of a landed nobility or gentry, whether the officials really separated their official functions from their wider social status and whether their power rested only on the former. These are questions to which we shall return in the light of later developments. Let us note for the present that administration, in theory and in practice, has a long history, that some ancient societies have seen the remarkable development and elaboration of administrative structures and of 'rational' bureaucratic procedures and administrative ideologies. In some of these societies they have seemed to stand at the very centre of social life. To the twentieth century, indeed, as state power and state activity burgeoned, such societies suddenly acquired a new significance.

22   Sally F. Moore, *Power and Property in Inca Peru*, New York, 1958.
23   Joseph A. Tainter, *The Collapse of Complex Societies*, Cambridge, 1988.

2

Rome and Byzantium

Ancient bureaucracy as despotism

The 'ancient bureaucracies' considered in the preceding chapter
were not the only societies in ancient and classical times or in
more recent Asian and Central and South American experience to
have strong states with sophisticated administrative arrangements. They stand out, however, as societies in which the state
played an unusually powerful role that extended beyond the
political to the managerial. They were not simply societies that
had a bureaucracy; they were, at least for a period, some of them
for millennia, profoundly bureaucratic societies, devoted above
all to management and control of the economic and social life of
their peoples. They were seen as such by their subjects and –
with admiration, fear or contempt – by those who dwelt on their
borders or saw them as different. Though appearing early in
human civilization – at the same time virtually as the invention of
writing – they were complex societies, both culturally and
economically.

Many anthropologists, especially in recent years, reject with
some sharpness the existence of a historical divide between
'primitive' and 'complex' societies, the pre-literate and the
literate, anthropology and sociology. One anthropologist, L.A.
Fallers, has written of Bantu bureaucracy under that title –
though perhaps, so far as that title is concerned, with tongue in
cheek. There has been growing interest in the administrative
arrangements and so-called administrative staffs of chieftain
societies and of some of the great 'medieval' African empires.
Much of this, of course, is a justified reaction against the
ignorance and dismissiveness that has characterized many
modern European attitudes to African and tribal and chieftain
societies. Such authors as I. Schapera and M.G. Smith have
brought out, for southern Africa and Nigeria in recent times, that

the traditional duties of chiefs covered much more than leadership and decision-making. A chief acted not only as legislator and judge but might organize agricultural activities and care for the needy, delegating powers to sub-chiefs on a territorial basis and bringing in personal assistants to advise and to carry out routine tasks. Some functional specialization was the result. In the area of Zaria in northern Nigeria from 1800 AD onward, in a much more complex society with vassals, successive régimes ruled and taxed tribal areas through a ranked system of chiefs, 'turbaned' officials and other titled officers including (Muslim) Koran-readers. Some of these posts were hereditary and some appointive; they could be held by freedmen, members of the royal family, eunuchs or slaves. But the powers of the ruler himself – he was not hereditary – were limited by custom and administration was strongly personalized. Lines of demarcation between specialized functions existed but horizontal demarcations were uncertainly drawn. There were no significant recording techniques, though writing was available through Muslim penetration, and much administration and decision-making was informal and consultative.[1] Recognizing that administration may truly be the oldest profession, one might still feel that this kind of executive responsibility is not sufficiently rule-based, does not involve enough specialized training and attention to records and precedents, and does not carry with it enough impersonal authority, to be treated as an example of bureaucracy as distinguished from a wider concept of administration, whether formal or informal. The distinguished historian of seventeenth-century English administration, G.E. Aylmer, tends toward a similar view:

it is hard to see how Weber's ideal-type bureaucracy or any conceivable variant derived from it (or in total opposition to it) can have any relevance for the study of non-literate societies. In this sense the England of Charles I or Oliver Cromwell, classical China and the modern industrialised states of the nineteenth and twentieth centuries must all have more in common with each other, and even with the eleventh-century papacy or the twelfth-century feudal monarchies of western Europe and the Byzantine empire, than any of them can have with most of pre-colonial Africa. Historians of

1 I. Schapera, *Government and Politics in Tribal Societies*, London, 1965, and M.G. Smith, *Government in Zazzau*, Oxford, 1960, summarized in E.N. Gladden, *A History of Public Administration*, vol. I, London, 1972, pp. 2–6.

witchcraft in Tudor and Stuart England have recently exemplified a fruitful and exciting interchange with social anthropology. Subject to correction, I doubt if the same possibilities are open to the student of administration and the civil service. If one were examining the impact of political and governmental action on the English village community, then an anthropological approach might be more rewarding.[2]

The point, as the last sentence suggests, may lie not only in the question of literacy. The Inca bureaucracy was not literate in the full sense, though the *quipus* did provide a basis for complex record-keeping. It lies as much in scale and in the extent to which the bureaucratic centre cannot simply accept, but needs to re-shape, the customs and traditions of local communities. It is this which creates the cultural 'greatness' of those ancient bureaucratic societies and empires, reinforces stratification at the top and gives earthly substance to the pretensions of their rulers. It is also a crucial part of the true official's sense of vocation and of identity.

Central to Weber's conception of bureaucracy, at least of bureaucracy in its most developed form, as an ideal type, is such a sense of vocation and what he saw as its elevation of abstract, formalistic rationality and impersonality. The regular activities required for the purposes of the organization are distributed in a fixed way as official duties. Operations are governed by a consistent system of abstract rules to be applied to particular cases so as to ensure uniformity. The ideal official conducts his office, as Weber puts it, 'in a spirit of formalistic impersonality: *sine ira et studio*, without hatred or passion, and hence without affection or enthusiasm'.[3] His vocation is the very opposite of the politician's, which rests on 'taking a stand' and 'being passionate'. Bureaucracy deals with the everyday in an everyday fashion; politics throws up 'charismatic' leaders who preach, create or demand breakthroughs, new outlooks and new obligations. Of course, politics too can become bureaucratized, humdrum – a tendency imposed upon it, as another great student of bureaucracy,

2 G.E. Aylmer, *The State's Servants: The Civil Service of the English Republic 1649–1660*, London, 1973, pp. 4–5.

3 Max Weber, *Economy and Society*, ed. G. Roth and C. Wittich, New York, 1968, vol. 1, p. 225. Also cited in Peter M. Blau, *Bureaucracy and Modern Society*, New York, 1956, p. 30.

Robert Michels, strove to show, by the development of modern mass political parties.

The bureaucracies considered in chapter 1 and some of the ancient writings associated with them, despite their patrimonial and religious setting, display in part even these features of Weber's 'rational' bureaucracy – impersonal and impartial behaviour as an ideal, the elaboration and application of abstract rules and the elevation of the rational–legal, of knowledge and education, including legal knowledge and education, as crucial to proper decision-making. They do so variably but to a much greater extent than one might have expected. Nevertheless, Weber himself not only recognized but emphasized the different social setting and the different conception of sovereignty and the basis for control in which and with which such ancient bureaucracies operated. Ancient bureaucracies were, for him, most commonly *patrimonial* organizations, a special case of traditional authority. Within such traditional authority, Weber distinguished *gerontocracy* (the rule of elders who represent the group and understand its sacred traditions), *patriarchalism* (where authority is exercised by a particular individual designated by a particular rule of inheritance but where his authority is still pre-eminently on behalf of the group as a whole) and *patrimonialism*. Patrimonialism, for Weber, is dependent on the development of a purely personal administrative staff and especially of a military force. *Members* of the society or group now become 'subjects'; authority, though it is still primarily oriented to tradition in its exercise, makes the claim of full personal powers. Patrimonial bureaucracy is thus regularized imperative coordination through a possibly very large staff, but its authority rests on tradition and its focus is the personal authority of the ruler. For Weber, indeed, that personal authority rests heavily on the external support of dependents – slaves, *coloni*, conscripted subjects, mercenaries, bodyguards and others. Where the patrimonial authority is freed from traditional limitations and approaches the arbitrary exercise of the ruler's will, the system becomes '*sultanism*'.

Patrimonial leaders or rulers may have had – in fact they did have – charisma which, for Weber, could be 'routinized', through their religious role and the pomp and ceremonies surrounding succession, so as to pass on to their heirs 'routinely'.

Though Weber does not make this point, there is a sense in which ancient bureaucracies routinized charisma in another direction – passing it on, as it were, from the ruler to his servants. These were also his representatives and thus shared in his supra-rational majesty. This was achieved – in the eyes of the populace at least – through investiture, designation, symbols of authority, participation in sacrifices and access to the ruler and his circle. Ancient bureaucracies thus elevated, at least to some degree, inter-personal, familial attitudes and procedures and religious cults. Certainly, as Weber emphasized, they failed fully to separate the private from the public – or, rather, they rejected the distinction; they often elevated situational ethics rather than abstract rules and substantive rather than formal justice; they used the absence of free speech and democracy at state level to act arbitrarily in relation to the population – though not to the ruler – when other circumstances permitted. The exactions they imposed on the rest of society were heavy and the role of material force, of fear and terror, in extracting economic surplus from the population and ensuring its obedience was great. Both slavery and the threat of slavery were of considerable, though varying, significance.

The power and efficiency, or at least the cultural and material achievements, of the great ancient bureaucracies were widely recognized and marvelled at in their own times, even by their enemies. They have continued to be recognized ever since. Among their neighbours standing on the fringes of empire – from Israel to the Greek city-states in antiquity – a distinctly hostile attitude toward them emerged early and became overwhelmingly influential at certain periods. Ancient eastern bureaucracies and their successors – the Persian and the Ottoman empires especially – served whole generations of Europeans over 2,000 years (though not continuously) as models of servile slave states, of oriental despotisms in which all, including the bureaucrats, trembled before the arbitrary power of an absolute ruler.

The Greeks and their classical city-states were well acquainted with tyranny as a form of one-man authoritarian rule resting on force. Such tyranny, as they saw it, might be benevolent or vicious and unjust – a matter depending on particular circumstances and the character of the tyrant. But in the wars between the Greeks and the Persian Achaemenid Empire (circa 559–330 BC),

Greek thinkers began to denigrate their Asian enemies by developing a new concept, that of 'despotic rule'. Despotism – for Aristotle, in his *Politics*, for instance – was the mode of kingship found among barbarians, or at least among Asian barbarians. It was based on an absolute and hereditary ruler; it was larger in scale and more durable over time than the forms of government known among the Greeks. Unlike tyranny, it rested on consent rather than force. This made it stable and even gave it a quasi-constitutional form, with recognized principles of succession. Constitutionalism was possible, however, only because the population of such oriental despotisms was servile by nature, or – no more than a hint in Aristotle, later a theory in Montesquieu – enervated by the climate. It endured despotism without resentment. The relationship between the oriental despot and his subjects was therefore not that between a ruler and free men. It was the relationship between a master and his slaves. In despotism, subjects had no rights *vis-à-vis* their sovereign. Yet despotism was the norm in Asia while tyranny was the exception among the Greeks. (The Jews took much the same view of Egypt – at least in those anti-monarchical writings that came to constitute the Old Testament, much as some of their culture and their literature initially owed to the Egyptians.)

The Persian (Iranian) Empire of the Achaemenids was a conquest state. Within a single generation, the Persians conquered Media (549 BC), Lydia (546 BC), Babylonia (538 BC) and Egypt (525 BC). They abolished the ruling houses in all four of these regions, but inherited significant bureaucratic traditions and arrangements. The third ruler, Darius, changed the political map by carving the Persian Empire up into twenty provinces, each governed by a satrap. He was careful, however, to preserve and encourage ancient cultures in order to avoid the hatred aroused by the earlier Assyrian Empire which had sought to destroy them. The satraps who ruled their provinces with a royal splendour encouraged by the Persian sovereign, the Great King, had considerable powers, the degree of their independence from the centre varying with time. Certainly, the satraps appointed the administrative staff that served them, hired mercenary troops and a bodyguard, directed the taxation of their provinces and commanded the provincial military levies. They even maintained diplomatic relations with neighbouring states. They were distinguished from vassal kings who were not satraps and from governors simply appointed as such. But to the Great King they owed absolute obedience, to be ostentatiously performed when demanded, and they were watched by him. Each satrap had a secretary who acted as liaison between him and the central government, reporting on the satrap's actions. The satraps, in principle if not always in fact, were governors rather than feudal lords or vassal kings. A central system of communications and intelligence, inspection by metropolitan officials with full powers and often their own armed force, the maintenance of Persian garrisons at strategic points and central taxation of the satrapies ensured or sought to ensure the military and physical dependence of the satraps. Though satraps normally served for long periods and could be succeeded by their sons, they could be arbitrarily dismissed or overruled by the king as Great King from whom all power stemmed and on whom it depended. In Darius's time, an imperial public works department had great powers and brought workmen to Persepolis, the new capital, from all parts of the Empire.

The Roman Republic

The bureaucracy that evolved in the Roman Empire and its Byzantine successor arose in a very different milieu, a non-bureaucratic republic that initially knew no absolute rulers and was founded on the expulsion or the myth of expulsion of alien kings. The Roman Republic was not a democracy. Its electoral system, even through changes, was always rigged. It was dominated, as Athens had been, by a struggle between classes – the patricians who ruled by right and the plebeians who sought and gradually gained admission to some elective offices, political representation and laws (as opposed to customs) that would guarantee their position.

The Roman Republic's legacy to Europe is not freedom or even the concept of freedom. Nor is it democracy. It is the elevation of law and above all of constitutional rules that govern and limit the exercise of political and administrative power. These rules and the extraordinary respect paid to law by the Romans were most probably linked with the earlier religious foundations of their institutions and of the rules governing the exercise of authority, including the central military and familial, legal and political, institutions of *imperium* and *potestas*. These defined, justified and circumscribed all properly exercised authority. The offices of the Republic – the magistracies (which were directorships, not judicial offices), including the tribunates and even the dictatorship – were political rather than administrative. All the magistracies, save for the extraordinary dictatorship and the position of general of cavalry, were elective. Magistrates issued orders and edicts in their own name. The basic republican conception, as Karl Loewenstein has put it in his *The Governance of Rome*, was that all power is delegated and that the delegation is limited in time and scope. Therefore, the Romans throughout the Republic persevered in the maintenance of two principles: the strictly temporary incumbency of the office and the equally rigid prohibition on holding simultaneously more than one elective office. The Romans insisted, from the beginnings of the Republic, on a determinate number of holders of any specific magistracy and on predetermined limited periods for extraordinary magistracies to be resorted to only in exceptional circumstances. To a startling extent, too, the Roman Republic emphasized devices meant to limit and control the power of the individual magistrate. Government was collegial not in the sense that official acts required a majority decision or that officials were legally required to consult and act jointly. Each office-holder was endowed with the full jurisdiction of his office. But every co-equal holder of an office had the right to intervene and veto an official act of his colleague by *intercessio*. Similarly, any magistrate of superior rank could intercede in the actions of officials in subordinate positions. Collegiality and intercession became complementary and assured unanimity. Without informal discussion and agreement among magistrates, government could not have been conducted. Intercession had to be undertaken by the magistrate personally through formally announcing his opposition to an intended act or cancelling an action already taken, but such a veto prevented or cancelled the act or action both legally and factually.

The principle, basic for Roman constitutionalism, that the public functions must be performed exclusively by ordinary magistrates and that extraordinary magistrates are legitimate merely for limited terms, Loewenstein reminds us, 'was departed from only towards the end of the republican era in the cases first of Sulla's and later of Caesar's dictatorships and finally by the second triumvirate (Octavian, Antony and Lepidus) to last for twice five years (from 43–33 BC). The violation of these basic constitutional rules signified the end of the republican system'.[4]

The bureaucratization of the Empire

Of course, as A.H.M. Jones reminded us in his *Studies in Roman Government and Law* (Oxford, 1960, esp. pp. 153–8), the Roman magistrate did not carry out his duties single-handed. There was a whole order of scribes – citizens, not slaves – who attended the magistracies and provided panels from which magistrates drew their staffs. The scribes appear to have been men of a certain standing as well as experience. Magistrates may have leant on them a good deal, both in accounting and in the judicial side of their work – just as Chinese magistrates and many magistrates today leant or lean on their experienced clerks. The grades of clerical and sub-clerical offices, Jones believes, survived under the Principate and, even as late as in the fourth and early fifth centuries, those in Rome were still asserting their right to assist in certain legal proceedings and to collect the appropriate fees.

As the republican conception of the magistracy was eroded and abandoned, the Republic collapsed. It did so in part because the republican constitution could not cope with an expanding empire. With that empire, a real bureaucracy developed. The two pillars on which the subsequent mature imperial system rested were the monocratic concentration of power (a process inaugurated by Julius Caesar) and a centrally controlled professional bureaucracy, holding the capital and the provinces together. The latter emerged slowly during the Principate, normally reckoned from the unconstitutional assumption of full powers by Octavian (later to become Augustus and first Princeps) in 31 BC to the accession of Diocletian (284 AD) or to the accession of Constantine the Great in 306 AD. The Roman Empire in the West lasted formally until the deposition of the last western emperor Romulus Augustus by the barbarians in 476. But in 330 AD Constantine

4 Karl Loewenstein, *The Governance of Rome*, The Hague, 1973, p. 20.

moved his capital to the east, to the city of Constantinople, the former Byzantium, where the Eastern Roman Empire survived many tribulations and changes of ruling caste or nationality for another 1,100 years, until its capital fell to the conquering Ottoman Turks in 1453.

Both the Persian and Ottoman empires as enemies and neighbours of Byzantium came to influence aspects of its political and bureaucratic structure. But already before the move to Constantinople the Principate as the rule of a *princeps civitatis* (leader of the state) had given way to the Dominate in which the *princeps* became *dominus* (lord and master – and, less plausibly, a god). Incipiently, he pretended to be absolute monarch or autocrat. The Roman emperors had used as one of their titles the Latin *dominus*. The Byzantine emperors adopted the Greek *despotes*. The word despot commemorates how much further they moved under eastern influence, toward the theory, if not always the practice, of the emperor as absolute and unchallengeable autocrat – a pretension inherited from them by the Tsar of All the Russias. (Against this, the Indo-European tradition of kingship since early times saw the king as providing charismatic leadership while limiting his powers quite significantly with the demand that he gain and keep the support and consent of the community through its leaders and independent institutions.) The Dominate of the fourth century AD has been described, with hindsight, as the end toward which Roman society had been moving for more than three centuries. It was probably welcomed by people of every class and station in the Roman world as the sole guarantee of peace, order and security in a society sickened by decades of foreign invasion, civil war and social chaos. The bridge from the Republic to the Empire, from the magistracies to the Dominate, was the bureaucracy that evolved between 31 BC and 476 AD. It did so with no little influence from Egypt and, perhaps, Asia.

Even in the thousand years after the fall of Rome, the Roman elevation of the independent force of law, continued by the Empire but born in the Republic, did have an enormous impact on the history of Europe. It has in modern times constituted one of the most important distinctions between European conceptions of a stable polity and of administration and those found in the great bureaucratic empires of the East, whether in ancient or modern communist times. To that we shall return. But in the thousand or more years that followed the fall of Rome, the bureaucratic traditions of the Principate and the Dominate passed to the East, to Byzantium, and, in part, to the Roman Catholic Church as a universal church, not to the new nation-states of Europe.

If we define bureaucracy structurally and say that bureaucracy exists wherever one meets with a hierarchy of positions which constitute the offices of an organization, T.F. Carney reminds us in an illuminating study of Romano-Byzantine bureaucracy, such a definition will encompass other bodies than the civil administration of a state. 'An army is, in these terms, bureaucratically organized. So is a church that can have a thousand officials associated with a huge building under an archbishop, and which includes archbishops, bishops and lesser clergy in a more territorially widespread disposition of its officials'.[5] In the late Roman world, indeed, church, army and civil administration evolved and became more and more prominent as major and complex bureaucracies, though always in principle subordinated to a constitutional framework with monocratic power, but not to a true patrimonial ruler until Byzantium adopted eastern habits. It is this which marks off the Principate, the Dominate and Byzantium from the Roman Republic.

The Princeps, as the highest official of the Roman people, from the beginning arrogated to himself the power to appoint the officials serving below him. In doing so, he was, at least in theory, subject in the same way as other citizens to the laws and to any agreements reached between him and the Senate. Some posts had to be filled by persons of senatorial rank, but lower posts in the imperial provinces and the entire administration of Egypt were barred to senators. The term 'procurator' was drawn from the administration of private households. It was meant to make it clear that these administrators were not to be seen as magistrates, but as assistants to the Princeps or persons empowered by him. The same applied to prefects. As Carney reminds us:

> The first *Princeps*, as the ruler of Rome's Empire and director of her government was initially known, could not wholly depend upon

5 T.F. Carney, *Bureaucracy in Traditional Society: Romano-Byzantine Bureaucracies Viewed from Within*, Lawrence, Kansas, 1971, p. 1.

the Senate, the aristocratic class which had hitherto run Rome's affairs, to administer under and for him. So he used the freed slaves of his extended household to perform some functions, and created new posts, for trusty creatures, to perform others. With governing powers increasingly devolving upon the *Princeps*, the functions (and numbers) of his various officials grew. Emperors came and went. There were four in one year in 69 AD, an unusually rapid turn-over. Imperial dynasties, too, passed away. The imperial officials, however, stayed on, and grew in effective (implementing) power, especially when the tempo of the game of imperial chairs was rapid or their holders incompetent. These officials regularized their positions, and extended and rationalized their functions. Hence the 'model' administrative bureaucracy of the Antonines, anonymous and competent. Then various among the officials came to be empowered over others (the Praetorian Prefect by the Severan dynasty for instance), so power constellations built up within the bureaucracy. Hence our word 'Pretorianism': by the third century these Prefects were so influential that they could make and unmake Emperors. Constantine dealt with this problem by raising another official, the Master of Offices, in importance; considerably weakening the Praetorian Prefect; and setting the two in a relationship wherein they inevitably conflicted with (and thereby controlled) one another. Justinian seems to have tried to do away with the built-up aggregations of power within the civil administration. He tried to make that administration into a series of minor functionaries and instrumentalities rather than a few large constellations of office and power. And so it went. Each of the bureaucracies was kept internally seething, as it were, in this way. If it was not departmental empire-building that was going on, then it would be power-plays or court intrigues. Morale and code of ethics varied with the fortunes of one's department, bishopric or unit within each overall bureaucracy. Thus the internal histories of the bureaucracies were records of ups and downs, rejoicings and despairings.

The balance of power between the various bureaucracies was no more stable.[6]

The Roman Republic had been brought down, at least directly, by the growing power of the military. The first Princeps, as Carney says, had changed the nature of the armies of the late Republic from political instruments of charismatic freebooters, transforming them into docile units of long-serving professionals, safe and apolitical upon distant frontiers. Of

6　Ibid., pp. 4–5.

course, there were ups and downs, reorganizations and an enormous increase, during the third century in the West, in military numbers and political power. By the fifth century, the military had become all-powerful behind a series of puppet emperors. In the East, on the other hand, the civil administration increased the number of military commanders and, by producing a situation of countervailing powers, brought them under control. Only in the sixth century with the wars of Justinian and in the seventh with the struggle against Islam were dangerous mandates of power forced upon the civil rulers in the East. These threatened the Empire from then on with collapse into an assemblage of feudal baronies. In short, in the Roman Empire, 'the power of the civil administration grew piecemeal in the first century, consolidated in the second, gained immense strategic importance in the third and developed into a mammoth bureaucracy in the fourth. It was to weaken in the West in the fifth but continued to be of central importance in the East for that century. Thereafter a diminution of its powers is probable.'[7] In the second century, it must be remembered, the Roman Empire surpassed in area the continental United States or the China of today.

Equally striking, or perhaps even more so, was the organizational history of the Christian Church in the Roman Empire. It began 'as a congeries of groups of believers ... with only the link of a common faith to help the faithful if they moved between towns. It grew in the second century ... into a flock guided and guarded by bishops with long range connections.'[8] In the third century, increasingly modelled on the organizational structure and divisions of that Empire, the church became equipped with doctrine, learning and bishops with powers of discipline and intermediacy. In the fourth century, Christianity became the sole official religion of that Empire – identified with the establishment, though at the cost of increasing dissidence in its ranks. By the fifth century, Carney stresses, the church was heavily involved in the world – an organized bureaucratic power administering law and vying with the civil administration and the military for power and influence. It was destined, however, to split into an eastern and western branch just as the Roman

7 Ibid., p. 6.
8 Carney, op. cit., p. 6.

Empire had done. In the West indeed, the end of Imperial Rome and the Lombard invasion of Italy (568–72) led to the rise of Papal Rome in which Pope Gregory the Great (r. 590–604) enabled the city and the Roman Church to withstand Lombard attacks while building an ordered church hierarchy under his control. By the eighth century, the Duchy of Rome owned extensive lands in central Italy and the Pope was head of a large administrative body possessed of enormous revenues.

Before Octavian–Augustus, the Roman machinery of government was decidedly unbureaucratic. It was the machinery usually associated with the city-state: annually elected magistrates, with a council of life members. Running the civil administration in the year 31 BC – the year in which Antony and Cleopatra lost the battle of Actium to Octavian – there was an annually elected hierarchy of forty *quaestors*, who acted as paymasters, six *aediles*, who looked after municipal affairs, and sixteen *praetors*, who conducted the business involved in lawsuits, together with two *consuls* as the top executive officials. Every five years, a pair of censors was elected for eighteen months to register citizens as voters in their appropriate tribe and order and to let governmental contracts, including farming out some taxes. Various minor posts comprised mint officials, officials to look after the streets of Rome and officials to deal with crimes among the lowly.[9] Even the army was officered by annually elected magistrates, though since Julius Caesar's campaign in 55 BC the legions had permanent numbers of 6,000 men divided into sixty centuries under a centurion and a regular promotion system. Six centuries formed a cohort and the ten cohorts in a legion were ranked in seniority, as were the centuries within the cohorts.

Bureaucracy, then, grew with Rome's territorial conquests, which by 31 BC rivalled those of Alexander the Great. Provincial governors, indeed, had a developed staff of *officiales* organized in grades from a *Princeps Praetore* (head of staff) to clerks, equerries and a bodyguard, permanently attached to the province. In 30 BC, when Octavian annexed Egypt, he forbade senators to enter the country, put it under an equestrian prefect with equestrian assistants and retained the Ptolemaic bureaucracy which had developed a complex system of economic regulation

9   See Carney, op. cit., pp. 29–33.

and taxation on the longstanding native foundations considered in chapter 1.

Behind the new arrangements inaugurated by Augustus at the very beginning of the Empire lay his recognition that he, as the Octavian who was an upstart Italian usurper, could not bank on the support or loyalty of the Roman aristocracy. Till then, that aristocracy had controlled virtually all the higher offices, which went mostly to men of the great families. Augustus moved against the Senate's treasury (*aerarium*) as the main source of government money by creating a new *fiscus* or pay-chest for each province. These henceforth paid only their *surplus* to the Senate's *aerarium* (from which Augustus could be authorized to make withdrawals).[10] The biggest concentration of funds was now in the Emperor's *patrimonium* or privy purse, into which the revenues of Egypt were incorporated. In control of the privy purse was Augustus's freedman accountant – a former slave who owed a client's duty to his patron, had no independent social or political influence and could be proceeded against with the fullest rigour of the law. Soon, another freedman was to control the Emperor's correspondence. The Emperor's treasurer came to control not only the mint, through more freedmen, but a whole series of subordinate bureaucratized shops associated with it. These were run by freedmen and slaves who procured precious metals, supervised contracted minting, put coins on the market and audited all those operations. An Emperor's household, as Carney puts it, had many mansions and the treasurer had a considerable staff below him consisting of freedmen from the Emperor's household. 'The higher grades were termed *proximi* (nearest to the Treasurer) and *mello-proximi* (destined to be nearest to the Treasurer), and had assistants to help *them*. The lower grades comprised cashiers (*dispensatores*) and accountants (*arcarii, tabularii*). A very considerable number of men seems to have been involved. Moreover the numerous imperial estates in the provinces were looked after by freedmen procurators, who reported in to the central Treasurer, but who each had his own staff of underlings'.[11] These former slaves, despite their apparent lowly status, were men of real power, running an apparatus state

10 Ibid., p. 36.
11 Ibid., p. 37.

with a redistributive economy in which wealth was obtained by
removing surpluses from primary producers and channelling
them around various governmental instrumentalities. Their formal salaries were low but perquisites were many and freedmen
could and did establish family fortunes. The Emperor made
further profit from permitting them to purchase their freedom –
usually only after they had produced grown sons to succeed
them.

Toward the end of his reign, building on the Board for the
Distribution of the Corn Doles established under the Republic to
feed the poor in time of famine, Augustus appointed a commis-
sioner with wide powers to charter necessary shipping, to look
after the storage of imported food and to punish dealers who were
tempted to corner supplies. The first holder of the office was a
former governor of Egypt, considered so able that he held the
post over a period of thirty years and several reigns.[12] The
mixture of organizing, executive and punitive functions and
powers that went with the office was typical of the system
Augustus was seeking to create.

In the army, Augustus broke the power of charismatic military
adventurers by placing legions at the borders in fixed positions
and deliberately intertwining military and civilian career lines
under the guise of restoring the Republic. He created, indeed, a
whole new set of official positions and career lines to go with
them by taking over responsibility for the provinces where
fighting was likely. This gave him seven provinces to the Senate's
ten and twenty-four legions to the Senate's one. The position of
legate and the post of procurator now became official steps in a
regular career sequence – there were legates in charge of a legion
and legates who were provincial governors.

The point about Augustus's innovations – carried out with
great political shrewdness – was that they succeeded within
seventeen years in turning the capital Rome, the most violent and
unruly city in the Empire, into the best policed and serviced city
therein. They improved greatly the competence and integrity of
provincial government and the professionalism of military command. All this was done without ceding concentration of military
power to senators and with careful institutionalized checks on the
work of senatorial governors and officials by equestrian procurators

12   E. N. Gladden, op. cit., p. 118.

or freedmen procurators of the imperial estate. The consulship, once the supreme prize and zenith of political ambition, became no more than a qualifying stage in the career system. Rome was divided into 265 precincts and fourteen districts. Italy itself was divided into eleven administrative regions. Central prefectures began to take shape – the Praetorian, the Urban and that in charge of the food supply. A central secretariat began with a minister of the treasury and, soon, a minister of correspondence. Two emperors later, Claudius was to develop the freedmen ministers into an enormously powerful central secretariat, adding a secretary in charge of petitions, a secretary in charge of enquiries, a transport secretary and a secretary on briefings to the existing treasury and correspondence secretaries. By the time of Hadrian (117–138 AD), the Emperor's council had become the key policy-making body of government, acting also as the supreme court and as the originator of new laws. Government finances had been extensively organized to diminish further the power of the Senate and equestrians had replaced imperial freedmen as ministers in the central secretariat.

The Antonines and the Dominate

Salary rankings in the 'model' bureaucracy of the Antonines that followed on from Hadrian, Carney reminds us, reveal the hierarchical nature of the apparatus, its formalism and its piecemeal growth:

> The lowest salary level, that of the *sexagenarii* (officials in receipt of 60,000 *sesterces* p.a.) comprised assistants of various sorts (e.g. the *adjutor* to the Prefect of the Grain Supply; the vice-director or *subcurator* of Sacred Buildings and Public Works). Here too were the assessors, *consiliarii*, of the Praetorian and Urban Prefects, the Correspondence Secretary for Greek, and the minor procurator-ships – of Pavements, for instance, or of regional parts of the Emperor's patrimony. Here also were the financial *procurators* of minor provinces, prefects of unimportant fleets, provincial *procurators* of the Public Post and provincially operating Public Prosecutors.
>
> The next grade up, that of the *centenarii* (officials on 100,000 *sesterces* p.a.), comprised the Correspondence Secretary for Latin;

procurators such as those of the Mint, Water Services, and Public Works – and the *a commentariis* of the Praetorian Prefect. It is a mark of the power of an official that his underlings receive preferential treatment and by this criterion the various Praetorians all bear witness to their master's preeminence within the apparatus. Also at this level were the Public Prosecutor, the sub-prefects of the Grain Supply and the Watch, and the financial *procurators* of large or strategically important provinces, of important fleets, of imperial mines and of big imperial estates.

The next grade, the *ducenarii* (officials on 200,000 *sesterces*), comprised those *procurators* who were heads of departments, or who served in imperial provinces of consular rank or conjoint provinces of praetorian rank. The topmost grade, the *trecenarii* (officials on 300,000 *sesterces*), included the Praetorian Prefect and the Prefects of the Grain Supply and the Watch; the Heads of the central secretariate, and the Directors of Finance (the *fiscus*) and the patrimony. [13]

Originally, such (tax-exempt) posts might be held for only a few years; there was no provision for a pension scheme. A succession of such, as one's career wound to its close, however, could make one's family fortunes. Pay was good and prestige was high. The expanded public services began to recruit officials from two new sources – freedmen and slaves who assisted the secretaries and procurators and army clerks, who staffed the offices of provincial governors, though Roman accountancy was in a primitive state and retarded by the awkward system of Greek and Roman numerical notation. The keeping of records on papyrus and then parchment drew freely on Greek and Egyptian experience. A system of shorthand had been in use since the Republic when the Senate had employed stenographers. State libraries, modelled upon the great library of Alexandria, had been inaugurated by one constructed for Julius Caesar.

The growth of the Dominate under Diocletian (284–305 AD) and his further extension and rationalization of the imperial bureaucracy have to be seen as a response to the military anarchy that characterized much of the third century. His greatest achievement, perhaps, was his reorganization of the financial system from 287 onward and the introduction of a new and stable currency. The indirect taxes, provincial tributes and testamentary

13 Carney, op. cit., pp. 58–9. Cf. E.N. Gladden, op. cit., pp. 121–3.

bequests, on which Augustus and his successors had relied as sources of revenue, and the irregular emergency levies and requisitions of the third century were largely replaced by a regular income tax on production and a capitation tax. The latter amounted to a wealth tax on rural property, including land, labour, crops and livestock. New taxes were periodically estimated and fixed and announced in advance; rural property for the capitation tax was assessed and brought to a common measure. As a result the government could know several years in advance what the approximate tax receipts would be and plan accordingly – though Diocletian did shrink, it seems, from ironing out all regional, social and economic differences and imposing a single uniform system upon the Empire. To combat inflation, he introduced an edict of maximum prices in 301, setting ceilings on over a thousand commodities and wage rates. Nevertheless, anarchy re-emerged. Twenty-six soldiers succeeded in their bid for the title of emperor between 238–284 AD. Rome's monetary system had collapsed; many of her provinces had been overrun, invaded or raided. Both Diocletian and Constantine, however, faced with the problem of administering a huge and diverse empire, had as sharp an eye to balancing the power of officials as to creating a rational structure. Thus Constantine created a Master of Offices to control the central secretariat in order to balance the power of the Praetorian Prefect, now responsible for army recruitment, supply of rations throughout the apparatus and control of arms factories. There were enough overlapping functions, however, to ensure a continuing power struggle between the Master of Offices and the Praetorian Prefect. By the fourth century, 'the civil administration of the Empire was ... divided into about a hundred provinces under governors, who had often purchased their post. Groups of provinces formed twelve dioceses headed by vicars. Superimposed on the dioceses were four prefectures, each under the administrative, judicial, and fiscal control of a pretorian prefect now divested of military command.'[14] (In deference to the dignity of Old Rome, she was allowed to retain a city prefect. In 359, New Rome also received a city prefect with less extensive authority.)

14 Enno Franzius, *History of the Byzantine Empire: Mother of Nations*, New York, 1967, pp. 22–3.

The professional bureaucracy developed in the Roman Empire was the first establishment of its kind in the western world. By accident more than by design, but also, one suspects, by imitation from Egypt and the East, organizational principles were invented which were in fact those used by all professional bureaucracies. Techniques were developed for recruiting officials, determining their emolument, status, promotion and retirement. There was education and in-service training. The bureaucracy was rigidly hierarchical at all levels, those of central government, of regional and of provincial administration. A hierarchy of titles, from *illustris* (one of them a eunuch constantly around the Emperor) through *spectabilis* and *clarissimus* in descending order from the top, reinforced the dignity of office. Chiefs of bureaux were classified, given seconds in command and supported by hordes of lower functionaries with specialized assignments – drafting documents (*notarii, exceptorii*), bureau assistants (*adjutores*), scribes (*apparitores*) down to messengers (*singularii*). The titles of lower officials were frequently and deliberately identical with those used in the army; the officials themselves wore a uniform in the shape of a kind of sword belt. On retirement, like discharged soldiers, they became *veterani*. Special administrative schools were attached to the central bureaux and separated according to their functions (training scribes, for instance, or at a lower level, process servers). Professional qualifications, however, were not required for entry into the service. At the highest level, appointment was largely political, at the discretion of the Princeps–Emperor and later, in the Dominate, by heredity. The recruitment of the vast mass of lower officials was centrally administered by a special office and only the special corps of the special police possessed recruiting autonomy. Nevertheless, posts could perfectly properly be bought. Usually a substantial fee was required and pocketed by an official on a somewhat higher level. Salaries of officials, especially at the higher level, were always insufficient, encouraging corruption, and were largely paid in credit slips for commodities in the imperial warehouses to beat inflation.

Officials were exempt from the most crushing taxes, however, and not subject to gratuitous performance of services to the state. Higher officials had to serve twenty or fifteen years, lower officials twenty-five. They were then entitled to a pension.[15]

The rise of the bureaucracies of 'oriental despotism' has been plotted, by many historians, as a story of economic-administrative imperatives. The development of Roman and Byzantine bureaucracy has been seen as displaying, at least equally, the overwhelming but shifting and often contradictory impact of political-military imperatives. The bureaucracies of the Roman Empire, of course, took shape against the background of military and political instability, at times accompanied by economic crisis, rapidly changing rulers or ruling elites and an empire whose territories and subjects, exceedingly diverse, could alter with bewildering rapidity.

All this was greatly exacerbated as the Eastern Roman Empire became a Byzantine empire increasingly cut off from its western sources. Justinian the Great (527–65) reconquered for a period parts of the Western Roman Empire from the barbarians and was probably the last purely Roman-minded emperor. Under his rule Africa, Italy, and southern Spain were recovered, a vast system of frontier fortification and garrisoning was undertaken, provincial administration and the economic and financial administration of the Empire were improved and Roman Law, with imperial edicts, was codified. His military achievements, however, did not survive him. The northern and eastern frontiers of the empire began crumbling under pressure from the Slavs and the Persians. The latter soon captured Palestine, Syria and Egypt. A swing of the pendulum toward Byzantium under Heraclius around 622 was halted and reversed by the rise of Islam and the Arab conquests of the Middle East and northern Africa. Meanwhile, the Bulgars became a constant menace in the north. Administration in Byzantium was reorganized for defence under provincial commanders who exercised both military and civil functions.

During the eighth century, Byzantium was saved by a new line of emperors of Asian origin and a century later, after a period of internal revolts and palace assassinations, a Macedonian dynasty launched the Byzantine Empire upon one of its greatest periods. In the process, the Empire, though always taking the historical

15 In these two paragraphs I have drawn on the summary in Loewenstein, op. cit., pp. 438–42.

and emotional link with the First Empire of Rome very seriously, came closer to an oriental despotism. The Emperor, wielding the power of both state and church, was now treated as almost holy. Court ceremonials, owing much to Sassanid Persia, emphasized the unapproachable character of the Emperor, even though he was for a period still formally elected by the Senate and the army. The administrative structure of the Byzantine Empire maintained its continuity with that of the Dominate, though the Patriarch and the Patriarchate grew in direct political and administrative status. But the fourteen ranks of officials came to be more directly controlled by the Emperor who himself conferred the titles of rank in a ceremonial audience and who had introduced eunuchs into the palace as a counterweight against influential high officials who might usurp the throne or covet it for their descendants.

The instability and orientalization of the Byzantine Empire should not blind one to its high level of education, aimed both at Hellenization of speech and mind and at specialized training for the professions, especially the legal and administrative. Constantinople, the Second Rome, remained the heart of Byzantine culture, administration and military power and a great city even when Persians, Slavs, Saracens, Seljuk Turks and Latins had largely dismantled the remainder of the Empire. Nor did its greatness come to an end with its fall to the Ottoman Turks in 1453. Under Suleiman (1495–1566), the Magnificent to Europeans, the Lawgiver to Muslims, the Ottomans saw the richest unfolding of their civilization and the extension and consolidation of an empire which covered North Africa, Egypt, Syria, Arabia, the Tigris–Euphrates valley, Armenia, Asia Minor, Greece, a large part of old Hungary and of modern Russia, and which threatened Italy, the rest of central and eastern Europe and Persia.

Both the later Byzantine Empire and the Ottoman have served their subsequent critics as models for the evils of unbridled absolutism and the consequent viciousness of palace intrigues. Royal brothers and sons were blinded or murdered by the ruler, wives incarcerated, daughters forced into atrocious marriages. Nevertheless, in its heyday, the Ottoman Empire was an impressive civilization. It ruled most of the Mediterranean world. It combined Orient and Occident and its Muslim mission of conquering the infidel and his lands with a specific place for its substantial Christian communities.

The laws of Islam – which were central to the Empire and limited the personal arbitrary power of the ruler – provide that conquered land becomes the absolute possession of the divinely commissioned prince or leader who commands the conquering army. The Ottoman Empire accordingly was divided into different landholding arrangements. All the land in Europe was regarded as state land, let out to Muslims or Christians under different terms. Asia Minor was also largely state land but Syria, Mesopotamia and Egypt were held under older arrangements and treated as tribute land. Arabia as the oldest Muslim possession was title land. The holy cities of Mecca and Medina, far from being taxed, were subsidized from the centre, but at the expense of tribute received from Egypt. The regions directly adminstered were divided into districts which had separate laws of taxation that rested on terms made at the time of the conquest. Of great importance was the deliberate maintenance or recognition of a belt of neutral or disputed territory around the Empire, from which the Ottoman people and government secured by raids a continuous supply of captives for the Empire's enormous slave trade.

The Empire rested above all on two great institutions, Albert Howe Lybyer reminds us:

> The Ottoman Ruling Institution included the sultan and his family, the officers of his household, the executive officers of the government, the standing army composed of cavalry and infantry, and a large body of young men who were being educated for service in the standing army, the court, and the government. These men wielded the sword, the pen and the scepter. They conducted the whole of the government except the mere rendering of justice in matters that were controlled by the Sacred Law, and those limited functions that were left in the hands of subject and foreign groups of non-Moslems. The most vital and characteristic features of this Institution were, first, that its personnel consisted, with few exceptions, of men born of Christian parents or of the sons of such; and, second, that almost every member of the institution came into it as the sultan's slave, and remained the sultan's slave throughout life no matter to what height of wealth, power and greatness he might attain.[16]

16 Albert Howe Lybyer, *The Government of the Ottoman Empire in the Time of Suleiman the Magnificent,* New York, 1966 (a reissue of the 1913 edn), p. 36.

The Christians who entered on their career path in the Ruling Institution were expected to be converted to Islam before they were far advanced. The children of such converts might adopt the same careers, but grandchildren were almost invariably excluded to maintain the flow of fresh converts.

The Ruling Institution comprised the state organization of the Ottoman Empire. It was copied closely by the delegated Government of Egypt and North Africa and less closely by tributary and vassal states. It was counterbalanced, in a relationship that was often one of rivalry, by the Muslim Institution of the Ottoman Empire. This second institution included the educators, priests, lawyers and judges of the Empire, all those who were in training for such duties and allied groups such as dervishes, emirs and descendants of the Prophet Mohammed. These men, all Muslims, embodied and maintained the substance and structure of learning, religion and law in the Empire. Greek, Armenian and Jewish Institutions were set up to parallel the function of the Muslim Institution for non-Muslim subjects within the area of personal law and communal organization permitted by the Empire.

The Ruling Institution, as Lybyer has put it,[17] was a 'school in which the pupils were enrolled for life'. Constantly under careful drill and discipline meant to train them for war and government, they advanced from stage to stage. They were rewarded with promotion, honours and gifts and punished for infractions. The ablest were put through courses in oriental languages and Muslim and foreign law.

The lifelong and systematic character of bodily and mental training in the Ottoman Empire, at least in its heyday, was made possible by the fact that all those being trained had the status of slave. But there was no disgrace in being the sultan's slave. It was the road to (delegated) power; it carried distinction and secured deference everywhere. It involved exemption from taxation and made the sultan responsible for the upkeep of the official, at least ultimately. The sultan, however, took pay for the granting of an office and in time every official under him did the same – a basis for corruption that was to prove fatal. Ottoman nobility and the high offices of state were on the whole not hereditary – the Ottomans, by an old Turkish rule probably derived from the

17   Ibid., p. 71.

Chinese, knew no nobility apart from office and public service (except descent from the Prophet).

The Ottoman Ruling Institution with its Grand Vizier, its Treasurer, and their staff of accountants and bookkeepers, divided into twenty-five regional and functional bureaux, its Chancellor and Chancery departments, under a 'divan' or council, was intended to maintain public order, defend the Empire against its enemies and carry out its sacred laws by conquering infidel lands and incorporating them within the Empire. There was, in the sixteenth century at least, a great desire to have well ordered intelligent government, even if its energies were overwhelmingly devoted to obtaining and distributing the means of its own support, to keeping its own machinery in order and to maintaining its authority within the Empire.

Structural versus historical approaches

All this history complicates, immeasurably, any attempt to trace the growth of bureaucracy in the great empires of the past as a story of simple and coherent political or economic, or even historical or structural, imperatives. Perhaps because the material for histories is often provided by bureaucrats or bureaucratic apologists themselves, it is tempting to see the role of ancient but especially imperial bureaucracies as that of providing the only stability and continuity in the midst of conflict, intrigue and chaos. That the bureaucrats often also added more than a measure of corruption cannot be denied.

The central theme of these great, but diverse and inherently unstable empires, the Roman, the Byzantine and its successor, the Ottoman, has perhaps been the relationship between centre and periphery. The ruler attempted through others to control far-flung provinces (often virtually nations) and diverse social groups – a situation in which the controllers, too, must be controlled. Here, there are internal 'logics' or tensions that at best complicate Max Weber's simple picture of ideal-type bureaucracy as directed to the efficient accomplishment of coherent large-scale tasks. The authority of subordinates, especially in the periphery, is greatly enhanced if they have local roots, independent local legitimacy and a high degree of autonomy or flexibility in making local decisions. But so is the danger they posed to the centre. One theme in all the bureaucracies we have been considering is the tension between central control and 'feudal' delegation or arrogation of local power. The result was not only central inspectorates, but a constant search for effective bureaucrats (and spies) without personal standing – slaves, freedmen, eunuchs, foreigners. Here, too, 'bureaucratic rationality' and the interest of the ruler required a delicate balancing of conflicting and competing desiderata.

Powerful individuals in the bureaucracy, provincial governors, satraps, 'warlords', pose a threat to the ruler, while indispensable for his power and authority over large and often diverse societies. The bureaucracy itself, if coherent and possessed of strong and independent *esprit de corps*, could also present an endemic threat. Roman and Byzantine emperors played off prefects and prefectorial offices against each other, balanced military and civil authority or attempted to prevent either from becoming separate and autonomous. Chinese emperors perfected the art of systematically inhibiting the emergence of long-lasting links between bureaucrats and the territories they administered by making officials serve outside their home provinces, transferring them to different parts of the empire as they rose in rank, and requiring at least temporary resignation from their office and return to their home province for extended mourning when the parents of the officials died.

There has been, in twentieth-century writing on past bureaucracies, a tendency to espouse either a 'historical' or a 'structural' approach. The latter sees bureaucracies primarily as arising from the need to solve certain very general social tasks – public works, tax collection, defence of far-flung frontiers. Such needs recur in different geographical places, in different historical circumstances and at different times. The approach to bureaucracy, therefore, tends to be comparative and often atemporal. If the search is for a general theory of bureaucracy, the tasks may be described in increasingly abstract terms – imposing the will of the centre on the periphery etc.

The historical approach elevates, to a much greater extent, the specific traditions and social conflicts in which bureaucracies arise, the changing circumstances in which they operate and the variety of distinct and often contradictory pressures and demands that shape their work. It is suspicious of the attempt to dismiss or 'transcend' the specificities of a society and a development. For the historian, the distinction between a bureaucrat and a local notable or aristocrat serving the king is not always, in all circumstances, as clear-cut as the theoretician likes to make it. Sometimes, it is not clear at all. Neither is the contrast between personalized and depersonalized rule and regulation in official conduct and ideology within the bureaucracy or in its relation to the people. Actual bureaucracies at all periods of history display an extraordinary intertwining of both. The debate about the Chinese gentry is a debate about the comparative importance of independent social position, wealth, etc., in the recruitment of the Confucian bureaucrat and its implications for the claim that the Chinese bureaucrat owes his position to state service alone. Similar debates have gone on over the *dihkan* in Abbasid Iran and the *pomeshchik* in Russia, both settled on state land in return for service, and over the satrap and the warlord. 'The historical fallacy' lies in missing the wood for the trees, neglecting the dominant tone and characteristics of a society by concentrating so exclusively or overwhelmingly on demarcation disputes that general description becomes impossible or inappropriate. That leads to historical misunderstanding. So does the attempt to assimilate imperial China, later Byzantium, the satrapies of the Near East or Islamic 'feudalism' to the feudalism of Europe with its fragmented and officially recognized competing power centres and allegiances, its complex interplay of established rights and duties, its recognition of the comparative independence of law as a social tradition and social institution.

3
Bureaucracy and the Making of Europe

Gemeinschaft *and* Gesellschaft

Weber's conception of 'modern', ideal-type bureaucracy as rational–legal in legitimation, structure and way of working is based, both consciously and unconsciously, on the history of Europe. The 'Protestant' ethic, with its elevation of sustained effort in work, of accountability and of a sense of vocation, is, for Weber, one ingredient. The rise of the money economy is another. So are Roman law and the Roman respect for law. European developments brought the 'Protestant' ethic, law, the growth of applied science and technology, and the use and pursuit of money together to create both the spirit and the reality of capitalism as an advancing economy. Its sources, of course, went back beyond Protestantism to the Benedictine Rule, to Catholic and Papal bankers and merchants as well as Protestants, to *agricultural* development and surplus, to a steady expansion of trade and – some believe – to the philosophical-religious separation between man and nature, user and used, that distinguishes the Old Testament and Greek-based European tradition from the dominant traditions of classical Asian cultures. But soon, capitalism also threw up new, wider, social problems, increased prestige for science, 'expertise', calculation and 'rational' planning, as well as the tendency toward the concentration of capital and the 'trustification' of firms. The entrepreneurial spirit of capitalism passed over, in the twentieth century, to an increasingly managerial spirit in organization, research and 'money management'. But that story belongs to chapter 4. In this chapter we consider the growth of royal and state administration and management of the nation-state, and its relation to feudalism and the later rejection of 'feudalism'.

Like so many nineteenth- and early twentieth-century thinkers, Weber saw capitalism – the commercial society of economic rationality (both of the individual and the firm), of efficient production and of the universal calculability introduced by money – as having wrought and continuing to work a tremendous and fundamental transformation in social ideology and human life. It created new bases for legitimacy and sovereignty; it radically changed social institutions and ways of working and produced different values and ways of life. Another German sociologist – contemporary with Weber but hardly ever mentioned by him – was Ferdinand Tönnies (1855–1936). In his classic *Gemeinschaft und Gesellschaft*, first published in 1887, he brought out the nature of the change in ways Weber would not have wholly agreed with, but which do help to illuminate what Weber and many others refer to by the term 'technical' or 'instrumental rationality' and what they mean by drawing the contrast between traditional and rational–legal authority.

Throughout Europe, or at least throughout modern commercial-industrial Europe, Tönnies thought, the authority of custom and traditions and personal relationships, family ties and communal sentiments and obligations were being swept away by a new commercial individualism that elevated the impersonal, the abstract, the traditionless. The city drove out the country; calculation replaced natural affection; the operation of law replaced that of custom and personal authority. Manchester economists, Whig historians and political liberals and republicans had celebrated this as part of the march of progress and rationality. They described and welcomed the late eighteenth-century shift from the authority of origins to the authority of ends, from the tyranny of man to the government of laws, from the dependence of status to the freedom, equality and self-determination of contract. Others, as the nineteenth century progressed, saw the liberation from 'feudalism' and the new industrial economy as threatening a new and more pervasive alienation and slavery. Already, at the end of the eighteenth century, Edmund Burke had lamented the passing of the age of chivalry and the new ascendancy of the 'sophisters, economists and calculators'. Money, Marx wrote in his essay 'On the Jewish Question', published in 1844, is that into which everything can be converted in modern bourgeois society. It makes everything saleable; it enables man to separate from himself as commodities not only his possessions and the products of his labour but even the very capacity to labour itself, which he can now sell to another.

Capitalism liberates 'economic man' (and greed) from social, moral and political restraint by dividing, separating, in the name of freedom, the moral, the political, the religious and the economic from each other. Formally, but not practically, it guarantees each its own presuppositions and the right to go its own way.

The capitalist order, the future socialist Chancellor of Austria Karl Renner was writing at the beginning of the twentieth century,[1] frees property from feudal and traditional restraints and destroys its social role as a continuing fund that constitutes a real and tangible basis of social production and social responsibility. The household, the Germanic *Gut* held together by the *potestas* of the *Gutsherr* acting as a provider and organizer of labour, justice and social services, is dissolved into a set of commercial relationships. The order of property, the order of labour and the general administrative order are no longer one: they part company as proprietorial power, managerial power and state administrative power. Where the social interest is *not* reducible to the operation of private interests, it becomes concentrated in the state as a 'public power'.

The enormous changes taking place in nineteenth-century European society occupied many of its greatest minds. Tönnies was the first to seek to develop the distinction between status and contract, elevated by Sir Henry Maine and the new sociology of Herbert Spencer, into a critical and professional sociology of the modern age, into an attempt to organize and understand the profound conflicts with the past and the new tendencies involved in the burgeoning 'bourgeois' society of contract and exchange, of commerce and commodity production. In doing so, he leant heavily on his work on Marx and his study of Hobbes, whose atomic individualism, the war of all against all in the state of nature, was Tönnies's model for the *Gesellschaft*.

Immediately Tönnies took his departure from the subtle differences between two German words. Both can mean a society, an association, a community, or a fellowship. But *Gemeinschaft*

---

1 J. Karner (pseud. for Karl Renner), 'Die soziale Funktion der Rechtsinstitute, besonders des Eigentums', in *Marx-Studien*, Bd 1, Vienna, 1904, pp. 63–192; revised edn as K. Renner, *Die Rechts-institute des Privatrechts und ihre soziale Funktion. Ein Beitrag zur Kritik des bürgerlichen Rechts*, Tübingen, 1929; English translation published as K. Renner, *The Institutions of Private Law and their Social Functions*, London, 1949.

tends or tended to be used of an association that is internal, organic, private, spontaneous: its paradigm, for Tönnies, was the *Gemeinschaft* of marriage, the *communio totius vitae*, the total sharing of a life. *Gesellschaft* – comparatively modern as a word and as a phenomenon – usually refers to something external, public, mechanical, formal, or legalistic. It is not an organic merger or fusion but a rational coming together for ends that remain individual. The 'secret' of the *Gemeinschaft*, for Tönnies, lay in the household and the concept of kinship, in the ties of blood, friendship, and neighbourhood. The 'secret' of the *Gesellschaft* lay in commerce and the concept of contract. Its ties are the ties created by the transaction between (abstract) persons; its measure for all things is money. The *Gemeinschaft*-type of society we find in the village and the feudal system based upon the village. *Gesellschaft* in its paradigmatic form is a society in which the cash nexus has driven out all other social ties and relations, in which people have become bound together only by contract and commercial exchange – that is, by impersonal ties. But it is also the society of 'rational' end-directed behaviour. Where *Gemeinschaft* is associated with the village, the household and agricultural production directly for use, the *Gesellschaft* is associated with the city, trade, wage labour and commodities production for exchange. Where Confucius elevated, as the mainsprings and patterns of social action, the five relationships of 'appropriate' duties – those between husband and wife, father and son, elder brother and younger brother, ruler and ruled, and friends – *Gesellschaft* puts forward the principles of utility and individual happiness – the greatest good of the greatest number as the sum of individual satisfactions. Where the first four relationships of Confucius are asymmetrical, involving status, the *Gesellschaft* elevates the abstract equality of the market, of people as buyers and sellers.

The 'common sphere' of the *Gemeinschaft*, for Tönnies, rests on a natural harmony, on the common acceptance of custom in the village and of a religious order in the town. The common sphere of the *Gesellschaft*, in so far as it exists at all, is based on the fleeting moment of contact within the commercial transaction – the moment when the object is leaving the sphere of influence of A but has not yet entered the sphere of influence of B. At this moment, for the contact to be successful, the wills of the two individuals need to be in accord, there has to be what the law of contract calls 'a meeting of minds'. It is a meeting which takes place only in connection with an offer and holds good only in return for a consideration. Money makes possible cooperation in means for the pursuit of separate, even conflicting, ends. Above this atomic, egoistic individualism stand only its two necessary guarantees – an abstract, impersonal system of law and the arithmetical summation of public opinion.

The distinction between *Gemeinschaft* and *Gesellschaft*, for Tönnies, is intimately associated with the distinction between two kinds of will, each characteristic of one of the two societies. The *Gemeinschaft* is based on the *Wesenwille*, the essential, natural or integral will in which a person expresses his or her whole personality, in which there is not developed differentiation between means and ends, between subject and object. Against this type of will stands the *Kürwille*, the instrumentally rational but in a sense capricious or arbitrary will developed in the *Gesellschaft*, the will in which means and ends have been sharply differentiated. In this will Max Weber's instrumentally rational (*zweckrational*) behaviour prevails. It aims at joy, profit; it avoids sorrow, loss; it is comfortable with none of the mixed joys and sorrows of non-commercial life. The first kind of will is expressed in our relationship to our children, our pets, the sod we and our forefathers have turned for generations; the second, in our attitude to the commercial share.

Gemeinschaft and *Gesellschaft* for Tönnies, more clearly perhaps for the later Tönnies, were not close, accurate descriptions of two different existing kinds of societies or historical stages. They are rather what he calls *Normalbegriffe*, an analogue of Max Weber's ideal types and of the modern concept of models. They are two opposed sets of connected presuppositions, two ways of structuring and seeing social reality and human relations, on which societies can be based. They are in that public sense, mental constructs (or rather selections). But they are selections derived from observable reality, suggesting hypotheses and lines of investigation in dealing with that reality and recognized as such by others. In an 'ideal type' or *Normalbegriff* some aspects of that reality are selected and accentuated in defining the type because of their apparent interdependence and theoretical importance. However, such ideal types are not, for Tönnies or for

Weber, classifications. No actual society or institution will conform completely to such a type. Tönnies himself likened the concepts *Gemeinschaft* and *Gesellschaft* to chemical elements that combine in different proportions. He made it clear that there was no question of treating even an institution like marriage as simply a *Gemeinschaft*. The point was to ask of a particular marriage or of a particular type of marriage-régime to what extent it approximated to the *Gemeinschaft* and to what extent to the *Gesellschaft* ideal. No one today would be unaware of the extent to which the public perception and legal regulation of marriage have moved from putting overwhelming emphasis on the *Gemeinschaft* element of marriage to converting it, formally at least, into a *Gesellschaft* institution based on contract, reciprocal rights and duties and the continuation of each partner's separate personality and individual satisfactions within the marriage. Something like that shift took place in public administration in nineteenth-century western Europe, replacing patronage, local status and the primacy of personal relations with numerically graded examinations, impersonal duties, definitions and offices, the growing separation of the office from its holder as a person.

In Tönnies's later work, including the substantially revised editions of *Gemeinschaft und Gesellschaft* he brought out at intervals between 1912 and 1936, and certainly in subsequent sociological reception of his thought, *Gemeinschaft* and *Gesellschaft* became more and more de-historicized as ideal types. They were preserved – but also criticized – by subsequent sociologists as polar opposites in a community–society continuum in which not only societies, but all sorts of specific human institutions and relationships, take up their positions. The US sociologist Talcott Parsons broke them down into four pattern variables that are polar opposites facing each social action with a dilemma of choice. These were *affectivity* (immediate self-gratification) versus *affective neutrality; diffuseness* (breadth of relationships, their inclusiveness, as between husband and wife) versus *specificity* (narrowness of relationships, e.g. between shop-assistant and customer); *particularism* (action governed by a reference scheme peculiar to the actors in the relationship) versus *universalism* (action in terms of generalized standards); and *ascription* (status-based evaluation of persons) versus *achievement*.

Max Weber was both more historical and less sympathetic to

socialism than Tönnies. He had studied ancient and medieval societies too carefully to lump all of them together under the heading *Gemeinschaft*. He was profoundly aware of the various forms of authority to be found in the *Gemeinschaften* he called traditional societies – *gerontocratic, patriarchal* and *patrimonial*, all of them involving more domination than Tönnies emphasized. Weber himself stressed the contractual presuppositions and realities underlying European feudalism. He was well acquainted with the strength of commercialism in parts of the ancient world. He saw modern capitalism as encouraging technical rationality, rather than alienation. He had no tendency to idealize the *Gemeinschaft* tradition or the traditions of *Gemeinschaft*, though he did feel responsibility for, and involvement with, the nation. Nevertheless, the trend of European society for Weber, as for Tönnies, lay in the shift from the personal to the impersonal in administration, from the authority of custom and tradition to that of laws, from the concept of the whole man to that of the specialized and efficient *functionary*. In true, pure, ideal-type bureaucracies, Weber believed, individual officials and the administrative staff as a whole are appointed and function under the supreme authority according to the following rules or criteria, which embody in each case (except in matters of hierarchy, of rank and status) the *Gesellschaft* as opposed to the *Gemeinschaft* side of the pattern variables:

1 Officials are personally free and subject to authority only with respect to their impersonal official obligations.
2 They are organized in a clearly defined hierarchy of offices.
3 Each office has a clearly defined sphere of competence in the legal sense.
4 The office is filled by a free contractual relationship, guaranteeing, in principle, free selection.
5 Candidates are selected on the basis of technical qualifications. In the most rational case, this is tested by examination or guaranteed by diplomas certifying technical training or both. Officials are *appointed*, not elected.
6 Officials are remunerated by fixed salaries in money, for the most part with the right to pensions. The salary scale is primarily graded according to rank in the hierarchy but the responsibility of the position and the requirements of the

incumbent's social status may be taken into account. The employing authority can terminate the employment only in certain circumstances; the official is always free to resign.

7   The office is treated as the sole, or at least the primary, occupation of the incumbent.

8   Membership of the bureaucracy constitutes a career. There is a system of promotion according to seniority or achievement or both. Promotion is dependent on the judgement of superiors.

9   The official works in complete separation from ownership of the means of administration and without appropriation of his position.

10 The official is subject to systematic discipline and control in the conduct of the office.

For Weber, in short, the rationality of 'bureaucracy' lay in its incorporation of *Gesellschaft* forms and attitudes. He called them not that, but rather 'rational–legal' or 'modern'. But subsequent writers have specifically linked his contrast between traditional (patrimonial) and rational–legal bureaucratic organizations with the *Gemeinschaft–Gesellschaft* contrast and set out that contrast in terms of pattern variables thus:

'Pre-modern' bureaucracies	'Modern' bureaucracies
personal	impersonal
traditional	rational
diffuse	specific
ascriptive	achievement-oriented
particularistic	universalistic

Weber knew that some 'rational' features were to be found in earlier bureaucracies. He distinguished, in *Wirtschaft und Gesellschaft*, modern rational–legal bureaucracy from patrimonial bureaucracy. In patrimonial bureaucracy there is a hierarchical organization with partly impersonal spheres of competence, but posts are occupied by unfree officials, slaves or dependents who, Weber says, can function in a (modern) bureaucratic manner only formally, not substantially. The trend in modern society is toward the expropriation of office-holders as owners of their offices (e.g. of church benefices), the replacing of elected officials by appointed ones and the increasing role of technical qualifications. Not only Weber but most historians of bureaucracy and public administration have seen administrative 'progress' in Europe (and elsewhere) and the emergence of the modern state as linked with, or consisting of, a shift from traditional, *Gemeinschaft*-like administration to the 'rationality' of the *Gesellschaft*, including its elevation of 'experts'. Tönnies himself, in his hopes of re-establishing a new secular *Gemeinschaft* through socialism, largely ignored the state and its power and the role of expertise. *Gemeinschaft* for him was formed from below, not imposed from above. But it has been argued by others that the individualism of the burgeoning *Gesellschaft* could only survive by transferring care for the public as opposed to the private interest to a specific institution with ever greater powers and responsibilities: the state and its bureaucracy.

The fragmentation of Europe

Both the idea of the modern state and the idea of Europe developed slowly. The Western Roman Empire had collapsed before the onslaught of Franks and Saxons, Ostrogoths and Visigoths, Vandals and then Lombards in the period between 406 and 572 AD. It left behind it everywhere in the West new societies in which small Germanic minorities came to mingle with Roman or Romanized populations. They were ruled by Germanic kings, comparatively independent of each other, who had set themselves up as great landowners, substantial farmers and great warriors. The Empire's creaking bureaucracy disappeared almost overnight, but its culture and traditions were long held in awe as the ultimate source of legitimacy. For a period this was re-inforced by the continuing prestige of Byzantium and the organization of the western church based on the authority of Rome and many Roman administrative practices. Nevertheless, the Western Roman Empire gave way to a mass of smaller states and principalities. As one lively overview puts it,[2] the Germanic invaders, in little more than six centuries, between, say, 450 and 1100, successfully transformed the western world from a centralized

2 I have drawn a number of ideas and vivid illustrations here and in the next few pages from Gerard Simons and the Editors of *Time-Life* Books, *The Birth of Europe* (Great Ages of Man), Amsterdam, 1985.

imperial domain facing the Mediterranean into a collection of independent and often warring kingdoms facing the North Sea and the Atlantic. Roman youths, achieving manhood, had been given togas as symbols of citizenship in an ordered polity held together in the *Pax Romana*. Barbarian boys, coming of age, received their first weapons. This continued personal reliance on the force of arms was rooted in the traditions and land-hunger of the tribes that swept into Europe from Scandinavia and central Asia in the great migration of the peoples. It left its mark on the face of Europe. It had enabled the barbarians to become both Rome's adversaries and a larger and larger proportion of her soldiers, helping to bring about her downfall from within. It then led to the fragmentation of the continent into hundreds of small independent states transformed into compact, self-sufficient strongholds that could be defended against conquest.

Slowly, this fragmented, increasingly agricultural civilization, wracked by internal wars and the need for each locality to defend itself, developed toward feudalism in its strict, European sense: the society based on the *feudum* or fief as the basis of political organization and of preparedness for war. The notion of the *feudum* merged the late Roman land-law concept of the *beneficium* with the Frankish personal institution of fealty and commendation (which had some parallel with the patron–client relationship that also became important in later Rome). The *beneficium* allowed a tenant the usufruct or part of it while leaving ultimate title with, or giving it to, another. In Frankish fealty a follower swore allegiance and loyalty to a lord or leader in exchange for protection, sustenance and originally a share of booty. The importance and distinctiveness of these *European* feudal institutions lay in the fact that the feudal relationship was a compact, at least in principle and in law. It was a compact between free men, each of whom had rights independent of and maintainable against the other.[3] Thus the fragmentation of Europe was accompanied

---

3 See, for a telling and succinct account, F.J. West, 'On the Ruins of Feudalism – Capitalism?', in E. Kamenka and R.S. Neale, eds, *Feudalism, Capitalism and Beyond*, London, 1975, pp. 51–60. See, also, Walter Ullmann, *Principles of Government and Politics in the Middle Ages*, 2nd edn, London, 1966, esp. at pp. 150ff, where Ullmann contrasts the unilateral nature of theocratic government with the essentially and profoundly contractual, bilateral nature of feudal government. Actual medieval kings, of course, tried to claim both feudal and theocratic functions and prerogatives – an important source of tension and conflict in medieval society.

by a certain persistence and mingling of Roman and Germanic laws as governing both rulers and ruled. There was, too, an even stronger persistence, at least among free men of substance, of the Frankish and more generally Germanic elevation of the dignity, freedom and independence of a leader's followers, of a lord's liegemen. And since the feudal society emerging in the ninth and tenth centuries was founded (conceptually, not historically) on a contract or an interlocking series of contracts, with an independent concept of law as regulating both parties to the contract, notions of equal access to the law and of *bona fides* or good faith were essential to it. This has been of crucial importance, at least in the past, in distinguishing administration in Europe from the great bureaucratized empires of the East – with the Roman Empire, perhaps, ultimately standing in an intermediate position.

It is now widely recognized that the so-called Dark Ages that were supposed to constitute the early medieval period in Europe in fact witnessed an extraordinarily vital and creative transformation of European backwaters, borderlands and overrun and ruined Roman provinces into a new Christian civilization. At the regional level, this transformation rested on new local alliances of king or prince and bishop. At the wider level, the Christian faith infused a more universal outlook and basis for communication. The church provided and worked out the social ideals and moral values, the political philosophy and the theory of legitimacy required by nomads and warriors still making the transition to settled agrarian and urban life. It furnished the trained personnel to sustain civil government; it claimed both to represent the positive heritage of Rome and to act as the king's instructor and then his conscience. There was no other agency, as one writer has put it,[4] that could have filled the political vacuum left by the weak Roman emperors and unequipped Germanic kings. Thus Charlemagne's claim to be 'Rector of Europe' required and gained the backing of the church. The church alone had a constructive attitude to society and an administrative organization capable of putting theory into practice. It had, too, a virtual monopoly of the literacy necessary for bureaucracy or administration.

The church, which had made significant gains in the last century of Roman rule, had an important appreciation of the role of bureaucratic structures together with a nominal subservience

4   Simons, op. cit., p. 57.

to the Bishop of Rome as the inheritor of St Peter's universal authority. But in fact, the church also had a strong tradition of regional autonomy that now stood it in particularly good stead.

Christianity was originally an urban phenomenon, and the first churches sprang up in populous administrative centres of the Empire. Due to their location and seniority, these centres (among them Milan, Bordeaux and Lyons) became the episcopal seats for the expanding Church and ecclesiastical organization was modelled after the Empire's provincial system. This arrangement placed the bishops in the middle of things, where each could respond swiftly to any emergencies in his district. As the Empire crumbled and its officials abandoned their posts in droves, the bishops were on hand to take over essential functions, and their experience at ecclesiastical administration equipped them to carry out their new secular chores with professional competence.[5]

The wary alliance of king and bishop, based on mutual self-interest, would remain an essential and pluralizing factor dominating European political life throughout the Middle Ages. So would the authority of princes, dukes, margraves and others at regional and provincial levels even as competing kings or emperors sought to establish more centralized authority over domains they had inherited or conquered. It was and remains a sheer matter of fact that no central authority effectively replaced the authority claimed and in part exercised by the Roman Empire in the West. There were successions of kings and dynasties – the Merovingians, the Carolingians, the Capetians, the Ottonians, the Hohenstaufen – but their power was generally short-lived and their kingdoms uncertain. Of these rulers, only the great Carolingian, Charlemagne, wielded his sceptre long enough and well enough to fuse vast areas of the continent into a cohesive empire. The Holy Roman Empire of the German Nation founded with the coronation of Charlemagne by Pope Leo III in 800 lasted formally for more than a thousand years, until its dissolution by Napoleon in 1806. Within fourteen years of its foundation it had united much of Europe under Frankish rule, but its authority was tenuous, especially to the East. The Empire became fragmented through division among Charlemagne's descendants and then through the incursions of the Vikings, Magyars and Saracens.

5 Ibid., p. 58.

Descendants of Carolingian administrators, counts and margraves rose to power as military leaders and formed great duchies. Castles sprang up everywhere; in Germany the Ottonian ascendancy was regionally limited and comparatively short-lived; the Hohenstaufen bid to re-establish royal and imperial authority in Germany, Italy and Sicily was successful for less than a century. By 1250 the Holy Roman Emperor could exercise his rule only with the consent of the princes. He himself was elected by an electoral body composed of three archbishops, the Ruler of the Palatinate, the Duke of Saxony, the Margrave of Brandenburg and the King of Bohemia. 'The Emperor became in effect the mouthpiece of the electors and the representative of the consensus which the electors had organized among the princes.'[6] By the sixteenth century, the Emperor was just one of a number of European potentates involved in frequent wars and shifting alliances with each other.

Germany, with the earliest pretensions to inheriting the authority of the Roman Empire, evolved, with Italy, into the most disunited of the political nations emerging in Europe. In the tenth century, Otto I (936–73), creator of the powerful German kingship that took over many of Charlemagne's pretensions, also continued Charlemagne's administrative use of (and control over) the church. Otto relied heavily on bishops, using them as royal agents but controlling their great wealth as well as their appointment. Counts were treated as royal officials, to be appointed and freely transferred by the king. The power of dukes as leaders of the great tribal duchies was thus undermined – some were expropriated on the king's behalf and some replaced or supervised by special counts palatine. Otto's son Otto II and his grandson, Otto III, continuing these policies, became Holy Roman Emperors and not only German kings. Otto III ruled for a period from Rome – though his pretensions, like his father's, were kept in check by both Slavs and Byzantines. In the two centuries that followed the growth of imperial authority was decisively checked by the wars which accompanied repeated conflicts with the Papacy. The last great protagonist of that authority, the Hohenstaufen Emperor Frederick II (1212–1250), whose French allies defeated the German Emperor Otto IV and

6 Reinhard Bendix, *Kings or People: Power and the Mandate to Rule*, Berkeley, Ca, 1978, p. 143.

his English allies at Bouvines in 1214, had inherited a more significantly bureaucratic system of administration from the Norman rulers of his Sicilian Kingdom and their Greek and Arab predecessors. In Sicily, he could tax his kingdom more thoroughly and regulate its affairs more minutely than any of his northern neighbours. But it would have been legally, politically and practically impossible for him to attempt such methods in his German lands. In France, in England and Scotland, in Spain and in other parts of Europe, too, dynasties with national support and national claims and aims came to the fore – though they were not clearly national until the thirteenth century. Before that, the seignorial household, self-supporting and essentially a personal unit of direction and management, was the primary power unit in much of Europe. By 1500, there were still several hundred more or less independent political units in Europe; not till four centuries later had they been consolidated into twenty-odd states. In that consolidation, the growth of powerful, hierarchical and centralized administrative institutions was a crucially important element. So was the sentiment of nationalism. National consolidation was to be furthered by

> an extraordinary complex of economic, political, social and intellectual developments: the invention and spread of printing; the rise of national vernaculars as literary languages, accompanied by the decline of Latin and other international languages; the revolutionary growth of capitalism and the middle classes, the role of aggressive divine right monarchs in suppressing feudalism and in consolidating and secularizing their realms on a national basis; the religious upheavals which eventuated in the disruption of Christendom and the establishment of state churches ...[7]

The subsequent elevation of a new sovereign, the people, immediately put a new problem on the agenda – that of defining 'the people' as a coherent unity and actually shaping them into one. Where Hobbes had seen society as composed of individuals under a person as sovereign, Rousseau saw it as composed of *communities*, each of which needed shared arrangements and sentiments to become a political entity. Political and cultural nationalism and a great expansion of the state's administrative

7   Carlton J. Hayes, 'Nationalism, Historical Development', in Edwin R. A. Seligman, ed., *Encyclopaedia of the Social Sciences*, vol. 11, New York, 1933, pp. 240–9 at p. 241.

role were the result – not only in finance, and economic matters, but in education, ideology and the supervision of social affairs.

The initial distinctiveness of Europe, nevertheless, lies in its fragmentation of sovereignty and of administration, at least in practical terms. Feudalism was neither centralized nor coherently hierarchical – a man could be lord in one relationship or in respect of one territory or title and liegeman in respect of another. Power rested not, in the first instance, on 'holding an office' but on holding a fief, though the two were much combined and the distinction blurred. The king in each polity – though this was much less so in Merovingian and Carolingian times – was not strong enough to control, let alone 'administer', both barons and church. His most important function, perhaps, especially in England, was as the source and ultimate provider of justice in disputes between lords and their subjects, between lord and lord, between civil power and religious incursions into it. Questions of administration in Europe were thus not simple questions of devising appropriate policies at the centre and feeding down appropriate commands and limited discretions through the centrally directed, coherently organized, levels of a command structure or bureaucracy. That the ruler might have done and did strive to do in China or Byzantium, not in medieval Europe. There administrative power and responsibility was fragmented between – ceded or delegated to – church, barons and municipal corporations on the one hand and the king's servants on the other. The king as such was confronted by privileges – ancient rights or liberties, grants and charters, titles preceding his own – and demands that he act within his powers. He was confronted by legal and not only practical limits to his jurisdiction. The European nobility had quickly turned lands granted in reward for service into hereditary lands, even if the king collected his cut as land passed from one generation to another. In England, the justiciar whose office met the need for an extension of the king's much more vigorous personal power in the period of the Norman and Angevin kings was the king's *alter ego*, for it was the king personally and not the king as head of an administrative structure who ruled. The need for a justiciar arose from the fact that England at that time was part of a continental empire in which other dominions required the royal presence in the same way as

England did. The justiciar fulfilling this role was exercising a vice-regal function in the king's absence.

The emergence of national administration

As England's administration, and especially the office of the Exchequer, grew in the reigns of Henry I and Henry II (the latter also reorganized the system of justice), the justiciarship came to reveal and satisfy an important second need. This was for a king's representative to supervise, even while the king was at home, important administrative and judicial affairs of the kingdom. These included everything that was done in the upper or the lower Exchequer as well as setting the Exchequer in motion and keeping its seal, the right to issue writs in the king's name, to control internal organization and to dispose over inferior offices, like knight, silversmith or melter.[8] This was the time when branches of the administration began to go 'out of court'. The Exchequer came to be physically and institutionally distinct from the single and undifferentiated Curia Regis; the Court of Common Pleas was similarly detached, though not decisively until Magna Carta. There was an immense increase in the keeping of records, and literacy became a primary requirement for almost all administrators, bringing clerics (even if only clerks in minor orders) to play an increasing part in secular government. Of course, even the society that had the only 'national' taxation system in Europe before the twelfth century could hardly have produced the Domesday Book (circa 1086) without a marked expansion and transformation of government – for the king, the *Anglo-Saxon Chronicle* tells us, 'sent his men over all England into every shire and had them find out'. These commissions of enquiry were charged with surveying all land as it had been held on the day Edward the Confessor died, recording the terms on which it was held, by whom, and its value. The commissioners recorded the number of cattle and sheep, the amount of woodland and land under plough, the names of landowners and peasants and the number of slaves. This was at first made necessary, above all, by taxation. Those features of feudalism

8 See Francis West, *The Justiciarship in England 1066–1232*, Cambridge, 1966, passim.

which made it effective in local administration made it equally effective in hiding the situation from the centre. Central administration did grow in England between the eleventh and thirteenth centuries and went on growing thereafter. But it was bedevilled by conflict – first by political conflict between the crown and the barons and later between the crown and other opposition forces. There were times when there was more cooperation than conflict, but there were also times of intense rivalry between what amounted to two or a number of administrative systems.[9] Much the same was true of most leading European states of the period.

France emerged as a nation at the start of the thirteenth century under Philip II, known as Philip Augustus. The Capetian kings had inaugurated a new phase by calling themselves Kings of France and not of the Franks and the victory at Bouvines let loose a torrent of national sentiment. Philip Augustus extended his realm – through marriage, conquest and confiscation – from Cherbourg to the Pyrenees, amassed a sizeable treasury, paved the streets of Paris and built the Louvre as a fortress to guard the Seine. He sent out royal agents from his court to administer local territories, collect taxes and try cases formerly tried by feudal lords. He kept such agents in a district for several years and reappointed them to other districts if they proved able. His successor, Louis IX, left local administration in the hands of the bailiffs (*baillis*) and stewards (*sénéschaux*) instituted by Philip Augustus, but sent inquisitors from the royal court to hear complaints by the people which would be reported back to the king over the heads of bailiffs and stewards. Philip IV (the Fair), ascending the throne in 1285, surrounded himself with ministers of state drawn neither from the baronage nor the clergy but from the ranks of law graduates. In Sicily, Frederick II as emperor had forbidden the nobles to make private war, excluded the clergy from public office and proclaimed the first medieval code to apply the principles of Roman law. He appointed trained and salaried officials to govern for him, but he failed to unite Italy with Germany and left no enduring state.

Both the nature and the extent of royal administration varied in

9   For a more careful chronological perspective on which I have drawn directly but without doing full justice to qualifications there, see G.E. Aylmer, *The King's Servants: The Civil Service of Charles I 1625–1642*, New York, 1961, pp. 422–39.

different parts of Europe and the kingdoms, duchies, principalities and prince-bishoprics that constituted them. But everywhere there was fragmentation and overlap, competing loyalty and competing jurisdiction – even if the state on the continent often sought more direct power and more direct administrative power than it did in England. Not until the rise of actual or would-be 'strong' and would-be absolute monarchs between the sixteenth and the eighteenth centuries did royal administration develop into something that might be called an administrative structure of central government based on stable and worked-over offices, regulations and rules of procedure. Spain, as the major colonial power of the sixteenth century, also grappled with the problems of creating an imperial administration. Still conciliar government and administrative execution through courts of justice continued to be predominant, with such rulers as Philip II of Spain attempting the impossible task of personally supervising and even participating in the very details of administration. In England, Thomas Cromwell, working for Henry VIII, was well ahead of his time in recognizing the need to create a system of offices that would function effectively irrespective of the specific incumbent. There was, indeed, what Geoffrey Elton has called a *Tudor Revolution in Government* – the formation of a Privy Council of leading offices and households, advising the king on policy but also concerned to execute and administer the organization of revenue-collecting departments and the speeding up of administration generally. All this began a changeover from personal to institutionalized royal government.[10] Even in early Stuart England – 'a much governed country' that yet had no standing army, no proper police force and very little central bureaucracy – it was possible to say as G.E. Aylmer has said:

> In the localities the will of the central government depended for its execution on the voluntary co-operation of a hierarchy of part-time, unpaid officials: Lord and Deputy Lieutenants, Sheriffs, Justices of the Peace, High and Petty Constables, Overseers of the Poor, and Churchwardens. Without their co-operation the central government was helpless: witness the failure in 1639–40 to collect Ship Money or to raise an efficient army against the Scots.[11]

10 E.N. Gladden, *A History of Public Administration*, vol. II: *From the Eleventh Century to the Present Day*, London, 1972, pp. 90–7.
11 Aylmer, op. cit., p. 7.

In France, a much more governed country, this had also been true, though Sir George Clark reminds us that 'the growth of bureaucracy – not its origin but its progress – was one of the characteristic seventeenth-century movements in most of the more thriving countries'.[12] In the post-Roman European world, indeed, it is only in the seventeenth and eighteenth centuries that royal administration takes on characteristics that at least point to bureaucratic organization rather than delegated and fragmented administration. It is in the eighteenth century that the term 'bureaucracy' spreads through European languages from France. The term was invented, it is said, by the French economist, wit and *intendant du commerce* Vincent de Gournay (1712–59). He was an important Physiocrat who translated such influential writers on economics (trade and usury) as Sir Josiah Child and Sir Thomas Culpeper. He also coined the slogan *laissez faire, laissez passer*. In a letter of 1 July 1764, frequently quoted in modern books on the concept of bureaucracy, the French philosopher Baron de Grimm wrote:

> We are obsessed by the idea of regulation, and our Masters of Requests refuse to understand that there is an infinity of things in a great state with which a government should not concern itself. The late M. de Gournay . . . sometimes used to say: 'We have an illness in France which bids fair to play havoc with us; this illness is called bureaumania'. Sometimes he used to invent a fourth or fifth form of government under the heading of bureaucracy.[13]

A year later, de Grimm wrote: 'The real spirit of the laws of France is that bureaucracy of which the late M. de Gournay . . . used to complain so greatly; here the officers, clerks, secretaries, inspectors and *intendants* are not appointed to benefit the public interest, indeed the public interest appears to have been established so that offices might exist'.[14] By 1789, the supplement to the Dictionary of the French Academy defined *bureaucratic* as 'power, influence of the heads and staff of government bureaux'.

12 G.N. Clark, *The Seventeenth Century*, Oxford, 1931, pp. 92–3, cited in Aylmer, op. cit., p. 439.

13 Baron de Grimm and Diderot, *Correspondance, littéraire, philosophique et critique, 1753–69*, 1813 edn, vol. 4, p. 146, as translated in Martin Albrow, *Bureaucracy*, London, 1970, p. 16.

14 Ibid., p. 508; in Albrow, op. cit., p. 16.

The word bureaucracy, clearly, had been derived from the term *bureau*, originally designating a writing table covered with coarse cloth (*bure*). *Bureau* was also used in eighteenth-century France (by extension) for the office in which an official worked. It spread quickly into other European languages, readily taking its place beside such widespread and widely understood designations for types of government as democracy, aristocracy, etc. It spread in Europe because there the phenomenon itself was both new enough to be startling and yet burgeoning as royal administrative pretensions in the would-be absolutist state and the size of public services increased. 'The growth of powerful, hierarchical and centralized administrative institutions in Europe', as Martin Krygier has put it, 'was a crucially important element in the development of the modern European nation-state and in the consolidation of several hundred more or less independent political units in 1500 into twenty-odd states in 1900'.[15] The increasingly structured and regularized (royal) administration in France from the early seventeenth century, in Prussia from the early eighteenth century and in Russia soon after influenced countries throughout Europe, though even earlier church, *Reich* and city-state had had their administrative arrangements and traditions. Confusion, competing authorities and responsibilities and – in many countries – a collegial system that was slow-moving and indecisive gradually gave way to centralized administrative direction on a hierarchical basis, strict division of functions and centralized recruiting systems with examinations meant to ensure professionalism. Administration, under the influence of the Enlightenment and then of the French Revolution and Napoleon, was rationalized, depersonalized. Royal servants became public or state servants as they had also done (more fleetingly) in the Commonwealth and the Protectorate under Oliver Cromwell.

The German word for an official or bureaucrat is *Beamte* – the man invested with office or *Amt* – and 'bureaucracy' can be and often is rendered as *Beamtenherrschaft*. The great nineteenth-century German dictionary prepared by Jakob and Wilhelm Grimm derives *Amt*, office, from the Latin *ambactus* (follower)

---

15   Martin Krygier, 'State and Bureaucracy in Europe: The Growth of a Concept', in Eugene Kamenka and Martin Krygier, eds, *Bureaucracy: The Career of a Concept*, London, 1979, p. 3.

but prefers the even then archaic German *Amtmann* (office-man or office-holder) to *Beamte* on the following, interestingly anti-centralist ground:

> In recent centuries the more beautiful word *Amtmann*, familiar to the people, has been replaced by the less expressive, more common *Beamte, der Beamte*, the sovereign's royal *Beamte*, he who has been given, lent an office, the *beamtete* which [construction] emphasises his dependence on a lord and which can also be stretched to cover all sorts of employees – military *Beamten*, tax *Beamten*, Chancelry *Beamten*.[16]

The Grimms missed the Celtic source of *Amt* and the fact that it originally expressed a personal relationship. Influenced by the Latin *officium, Amt* came, in the period of the Roman Empire, to mean 'office', *officium*, in the sense in which Augustus had created such offices to stand beside the magistracies. In this sense, it merged with incorporeal hereditaments, *honor* and *beneficium*. Not till the sixteenth century in Germany did protest against the heritability of offices gain momentum.

A rapid increase in the centralization of military and administrative power indeed made itself evident in much of Europe in the seventeenth and eighteenth centuries. It was the age of actual or would-be absolutism, of the merger between dynastic and national ambitions and of mercantilism, of the concern with wealth as the basis of state power and the consequent regulation of imports, navigation, reclamation of land and rulers' interest in attracting skilled migrants. A multitude of internal markets, it was believed, should be coalesced into one national market; colonies should be acquired and exploited for raw materials; local administration would have to give way to national administration. The church, corporations and estates, local aristocrats and provincial capitals, and far-flung colonies, would become subordinate to power exercised from the centre. Slowly, at a very uneven pace if one compares the various countries of Europe, and with a significant boost from Protestantism and the formation of national churches, this is what happened. The ever-more centralized

---

16   J. and W. Grimm, *Deutsches Wörterbuch*, Leipzig, 1854. The German prefix *be* makes the concept that follows passive or transitive – it elevates a process of endowing, not of making or being.

royal administration in seventeenth- and eighteenth-century Europe gave way after the French Revolution and Napoleon to a concept of *public* administration.

Rationalizing administration: France

The growth of bureaucracy in seventeenth, eighteenth and even nineteenth-century Europe is associated, especially, with France, Prussia, Austria and Russia – great powers that were becoming or striving to become greater. A part and perhaps a necessary precondition of their greatness militarily, politically, culturally and economically, lay in the effective supremacy of their rulers over internal and external challengers. The crown needed, though it did not always get, money, obedience and unrivalled supreme authority within its realm. This was the making of the nation-state. Thus, Louis XI, Louis XII and Francis I, in France between 1461 and 1547, promoted centralizing policies and administrative reforms. In the two latter reigns, those Masters of Requests charged with exercising general control of financial administration were singled out as *intendants* of finance and elevated above the other Masters to be given seats in the *Conseil d'Etat*. In the reigns of Henry III (1575–89) and Henry IV (1589–1610), the extraordinary commissions established to collect the *taille* (the direct tax levied for the King) were being regularized as 'provincial *intendants*'. Though not permanent officials attached to the province, they were called upon to supervise dissident elements in the provinces and to organize public relief in times of hardship. Soon, there were some thirty of them. They advised the King on local fiscal, military and administrative problems. They supervised and inspected local officials. They enforced or sought to enforce laws that were being flouted.

Under Louis XIII, a weak and idle King content to let Richelieu the Cardinal-administrator of brilliance exercise power in his name, central administration and royal authority grew stronger, though they remained intensely personal, exercised on behalf of the King through Richelieu and, after Richelieu's death in 1642 and the accession of Louis XIV as a child two years later, by Cardinal Mazarin. Both men worked tirelessly and brilliantly to help the Bourbons replace the Habsburgs and France replace Spain as the leading power in Europe. Vigorously promoting the King's cause against the nobility, they attempted in various ways to gain the support of the middle class and to bring it into administration. Between 1634 and 1648, *intendants* had been sent to almost every *generalité* in France; by the mid-seventeenth century, the *intendants* supervised 'the assessment and collection of royal taxes, the organization of local police or militia, the preservation of order and the conduct of courts'.[17] As Roland Mousnier puts it, 'from an inspector-reformer, the provincial *intendant* [became] an administrator',[18] supported by a staff of subordinate officials.

Mazarin, during the minority of Louis XIV, pursuing Richelieu's centralizing policies, met with strong opposition from local officials and the middle classes, which brought about the *Frondes* disturbances between 1648 and 1653. The *Frondes* had sought to renew the hereditary possession of office in certain law courts, to abolish the office of *intendants* everywhere except in border regions and to declare financial edicts illegal if they were not registered by the Paris *parlements* (courts).

The *Frondes* were suppressed and the *intendants* gradually reintroduced, though there was some royal and ministerial concern with limiting their power and scope of activity. Louis XIV took personal charge of the kingdom after Mazarin's death in 1661 and appointed the mercantilist Jean-Baptiste Colbert as Chief Minister. Colbert, like Louis XIV himself, vigorously pursued the Richelieu/Mazarin policy of seeking to make the King the sole authority in the kingdom especially in finance, politics and military affairs. Louis's frequent wars, his determination to preserve the unity and further the greatness of the French state, and the administrative interests and ambitions of Colbert worked in favour of centralization. The policy was ideologized in Bishop Bossuet's theory of divine kingship which ascribed to the King sacredness of person, a paternal relationship to his people, absolute power that made him accountable to God alone and greater reason than that given to ordinary mortals. For

17   Carlton J. Hayes, *A Political and Cultural History of Modern Europe*, rev. edn, vol. 1, New York, 1932, p. 284.

18   Roland Mousnier, *La Plume, la faucille et le marteau*, Paris, 1970, p. 181; cited by Krygier, 'State and Bureaucracy', pp. 3–4.

Bossuet, who became tutor to the future Louis XV, the power of all individuals in the community was united in the King as a public person in whom the nation is embodied. Thus, royal administration became stronger and stronger but remained intensely personal. Ministers after 1661 were appointed by verbal command and there were never more than five at any one time. The secretaries of state sat with the Chancellor as chief representatives of the King in the councils. A controller-general of finances was created in 1665, a post filled by Colbert himself, who had been *intendant* of finances in the Council of Finances since 1661. He had direction of agriculture, general industry, domestic and foreign commerce and colonies. As superintendent of buildings, he was also responsible for royal buildings and royal arts and manufactures. A *Conseil des Dépeches* served as the chief administrative body of the kingdom; another council, the *Conseil d'Etat*, reduced to four or five members besides the king, dealt with all great affairs of the state and acted as the highest court of appeal in civil or administrative matters. A Council of Finances or Royal Council fixed taxes and supervised tax farming.

The vast majority of offices, however – though not that of *intendant* or those of his subordinates – remained, like tax collection, a form of property. The tax farmers on whom the crown depended could be controlled only by occasional legal process, not by continuous administrative direction. Privilege, *grâces*, favours and marks of distinction consisted in personal exemptions and exceptions.[19] With the accession of Louis XV, the situation worsened; conflict, venality and self-seeking increased. Franklin L. Ford writes:

The structure of French government in the eighteenth century has been variously described by a series of metaphors, all of them designed to convey the impression of a complexity bordering on utter confusion. Behind this situation lay the long process of accretion inherent in the crown's efforts to maintain control of its unavoidable delegations of authority. By the time of Louis XV, that process had produced a bewildering array of governmental organs, many of them fallen into contempt and near uselessness, but each

19 See J.F. Bosher, *French Finances 1770–1795: From Business to Bureaucracy*, Cambridge, 1970, pp. xii, 277, cited by Krygier, 'State and Bureaucracy', p. 5.

still asserting its claim to control over some portion of the conduct, the personal property, the taxes, the disputes or the physical services of the French population ... Moreover, the effects of the long reign just ended were apparent in the tremendously over-expanded bureaucracy, swelled by the thousands of sinecures which the government had sold to increase its monetary income.[20]

The French Revolution, elevating the people as sovereign and the public welfare as the end of government, transformed the situation. The state and state authority were depersonalized; royal officials became public employees or functionaries, paid by the state and responsible to the nation or its representatives. Initially, the Constituent Assembly was federative and decentralizing. It divided the country into eighty-three departments, each administered by a General Council of thirty-six members elected on a restricted franchise. Each General Council designated a Directorate of eight to act as its executive arm, to oversee the issuing of regulations and the administration of finances and to take over the archives of the *intendants*. (In the provinces, where literacy was poor, the task proved beyond those charged with it.) Day-to-day administration was delegated to the districts, centres and municipalities or communes, working under elected mayors. Some of their functions were allocated to them by law, some delegated to them from above.

The liberal phase of the Revolution ended on 10 August, 1792, with the sack of the Tuileries, the suspension of the King and the inauguration of the Terror. Increasing chaos, the execution of the King, civil war within and patriotic war outside produced a new Convention, the declaration of the Republic, the intensification of the Terror and increasing authoritarian control by what amounted to ministries of police, first the Council of General Security and then, after April 1793, the Committee of Public Safety. The latter began by supervising the work of the Council of Ministers and then took over complete executive responsibilities, except those over finances.

The experiments in local self-government initiated by the Revolution failed both practically and under attacks from bourgeois and Jacobins alike. The centralizing authoritarianism

20   Franklin L. Ford, *Robe and Sword: The Regrouping of the French Aristocracy after Louis XIV*, New York, 1965, pp. 35–6, cited in Krygier, 'State and Bureaucracy', p. 4.

of the Convention was to survive, even if the Terror did not. Napoleon kept and strengthened the centralized administrative structure. His prefects, appointed by him and under strong central control, governed the provinces through *conseils*, sub-prefects and the mayors of communes. They have been described by Richard Cobb as unattractive, efficient and featureless bureaucrats, professional administrators forming a strong contrast with the *sans-culotte* prefects of the Revolution and the amateurs of the easy-going Bourbon Restoration. They were, Cobb notes, young, thrusting, vigorous, ambitious and unquestioning. In Napoleon's Empire, too, police organization was perfected. A Ministry of General Police was organized into functional divisions. One supervised commerce, health and highways; another surveillance and security (including secret police); a third custom and opinion, as well as immigrants; a secretariat opened all dispatches and reported to the Minister on matters reserved for him. By 1811, 130 *commissaires généraux* carried out all the regulatory functions of an old-fashioned police state in the larger cities, while *commissaires de police* did this in smaller towns. Charity was organized by Charity Offices and a Central Commission under the Minister of the Interior. Workhouses and hospitals were set up or run in a similar way. Primary and secondary schools were placed under the supervision of the Ministry of the Interior and its Director of Public Instruction, though the state's general monopoly of education was relaxed after 1806. An Imperial University was established in that year and Faculties of Law were encouraged by the Empire's administrators. A whole structure of administrative law and administrative appeal with its own court system was created. Centralization, especially administrative centralization, provided the link between the France of Louis XIV and that of Napoleon. Enormously strengthened by the shift to more impersonal, public administration, it survived Restoration amateurism and the temporary recovery of the provincial nobility to become the hallmark of French public life.

The rise of Prussia

Prussia, the historian Sir Lewis Namier insisted in one of his more generalizing and anti-German moods, was not a state but a military-administrative machine, ready and able to rule diverse peoples, shift populations and expand its territory whenever opportunity offered. The rise of the Hohenzollern from obscurity in the small Electorate of Brandenburg to growing pre-eminence among German princes was based on their willingness, in the seventeenth and eighteenth centuries, to break with old forms and concepts of government, to pursue the twin goals of military discipline and centralized direction. They thus created and boasted of being 'the Sparta of the North'. The Hohenzollern achieved this in spite of the fact that Prussia had been poor, depopulated, and dominated, after the decisive defeat of the Teutonic Order in the middle of the fifteenth century, by Poland and then by Sweden. Its nobility, arrogant and powerful, consolidated its demesne farms in the seventeenth and eighteenth centuries into large arable estates and reduced the peasantry to serfdom.

The expansion of Prussian power in the seventeenth and eighteenth centuries took place through strong administration, though the Hohenzollern were 'the rulers of a string of heterogeneous principalities scattered across the northern parts of Germany from Poland to the Netherlands',[21] not hereditary autocrats in an already unified state. Elector Frederick William of Brandenburg (1640–88), the Great Elector, had persuaded Sweden to recognize his rule over Brandenburg–Prussia and made it the largest German polity next to the lands of the House of Habsburg, but he was still not king. The first King in Prussia, Frederick I (1688–1713), needed Imperial approval to crown himself (in Königsberg, now Kaliningrad) in 1701. His lands were a collection of estates, provinces and other feudal entities. He was, as Hans Rosenberg reminds us, not only King of Prussia, but at the same time Elector of Brandenburg, Duke of Pomerania, Magdeburg, Cleves, and (after 1740) Silesia, Prince of Halberstadt and Minden, Count of Mark and Ravensberg, etc. Not until the First Partition of Poland did the 'King *in* Prussia' become 'King *of* Prussia' by acquiring the western parts of the territory of the 'ancient Prussians' – that is, regaining the lands acquired by the Teutonic Order and ceded to Poland in the fifteenth century. Yet in the eighteenth and early nineteenth

21 Hans Rosenberg, *Bureaucracy, Aristocracy and Autocracy: The Prussian Experience 1660–1815*, Cambridge, Mass., 1958, p. 27.

century, the aggressive Prussian frontier state emerged as a future leader of Germany, with the most professionalized and disciplined public service in Europe. Three men – the Great Elector Frederick William of Brandenburg, King Frederick William I (r. 1713–40) and Frederick II (the Great, r. 1740–86) – stood at the centre of this remarkable growth. Their success rested on opportunism, military discipline and their readiness to draw on absolutist methods, professional skills and people shaped in and outside the wider Germany. The Great Elector had set out to convert a *Territorialstaat* based on personal union into a *Gesamtstaat* (a unified state) by subordinating the princes and the administrative organs of the territories to his central authority. He achieved this on a pretext, the need for perpetual military mobilization, failing to disband his armies when the Peace of Olivia terminated the Swedish–Polish war. In 1651, he reconstructed the Brandenburg Privy Council, dividing its business among colleges of Councillors, to weaken the territorial principle. He transformed the earlier war commissars into administrative agents blending military and civil authority and subjected social and economic life to increasing regimentation.[22]

Frederick William I consolidated the system in which, during the inconclusive political interlude between 1688 and 1713, impermanent cliques of courtiers had exercised state power while the permanently organized civil bureaucracy acquired massive strength. He first divided Prussia and its administration more clearly into two distinct administrative groupings – the civil and the military – and then established, in 1723, a single supreme administrative body to control both – the General Directory to which local estates, corporations and courts became subordinate. The General Directory was responsible for finance, war and domains. The King became its President. There were five vice-presidents or directing ministers, running four departments. They were collectively responsible to the King. Under them were fourteen finance, war and domain councillors, responsible only for what was done in their specific departments. The Directory

22 See Otto Hintze, 'Der Österreichische und der preussische Beamtenstaat im 17. und 18. Jahrhundert', in his *Staat und Verfassung* (Gesammelte Abhandlungen, Bd I), 3., durchges. u. erweit. Aufl., Göttingen, 1962, pp. 321–58; Gustav Schmoller, *Deutsches Städtewesen in älterer Zeit*, Bonn and Leipzig, 1922, pp. 415–25; Reinhold August Dorwart, *The Administrative Reforms of Frederick William I of Prussia*, Cambridge, Mass., 1953, pp. 3–4, and Hans Rosenberg, op. cit., pp. 34–7.

was to meet every Monday, Wednesday, Thursday and Friday, reserving one day each for collegial discussion of the work of the four departments. It also discussed the work of the Audit Office and judicial affairs, which were supervised by the fifth minister. The affairs of fifteen legally distinct provinces, from Prussia, Pomerania and Neumark to Minden, Ravensberg and the Orange Succession lands, were discussed as specific questions, but conduct of these affairs was distributed among the departments. The King, in an Instruction establishing the General Directory, declared that he would show his special, constant and untiring attention to its affairs and directed the five ministers to search, when servants of the directory were needed, for such

> able people as can be found, either of Reformed or Lutheran Confession, loyal and honest, open-minded, who understand economy and have good knowledge of commerce and manufacturing, who can write, above all are our native subjects, though we would accept one or two exceptionally able foreigners into our General Directory. To sum up briefly the above qualities, they must be such people as are capable of everything for which one wants to use them. [23]

In the provincial organs the appointees were to be native to the province, good and experienced managers. The posts of collectors of town dues, mill inspectors, police inspectors and gendarmes were to be reserved for non-commissioned officers and soldiers or military invalids.

As in so many monocratic administrations, the system was further supervised by secret agents – the Minister of State, Moritz von Viebahn, was given the task of making confidential reports to the king or other ministers and the *fiscals* were formed into a separate small hierarchy, acting both as administrative police or inspectors and as public prosecutors. [24]

Prussia, the first nation in Europe to introduce general examination for the civil service, had by 1700 already instituted examinations for military judges and judicial counsellors. Frederick William established chairs of Cameralistics at Halle and Frankfurt in 1727 to give instruction in 'the principles of

---

23 As translated in Dorwart, op. cit., Appendix, p. 200.
24 Cf. E.N. Gladden, op. cit., vol. 11, p. 161.

agriculture and police, also the institution of surveys of offices and estates, and also the efficient administration and government of towns'.[25] Successful candidates were to serve in departments on an unpaid basis to acquire experience before being given permanent appointment. Much emphasis, too, was put on their moral character – a matter of concern to the King.

Poorly paid but regularly, not especially well educated, operating in a climate where perquisites and personal favours were still usual, Prussian officials nevertheless attained a reputation for devotion to duty and high moral character jealously watched over by the King and his fiscals. The personality of Frederick William I itself had great influence, as did that of his son, Frederick the Great. Initially suspicious of the power of Prussia's bureaucratic elite, but much more open to Enlightenment influence from France, the new King at first reduced the powers of the General Directory. But in his reign, Prussia became a major European power, at the zenith of its eighteenth-century military and political power. It was unified, in spite of or because of war and territorial expansion, by a strong standing army and its *Junker* officer class, ruthless economy in government and a king dedicated to serving the state. The ranks of officialdom grew and continued to grow, the range of their functions increased.

[By 1770] . . . the General Directory's chief minister, von Hagen, had persuaded Frederick to support the establishment of a centralized recruiting system for the whole executive corps of the bureaucracy, and in February 1770 a Superior Examination Commission began to operate. . . . By the end of the century a merit system applied to all posts; a degree in cameralistics was required for higher posts, followed by a period of practical training and a further oral and written examination.[26]

The reign of Frederick the Great, for all its and his brilliance, is generally seen by historians of Prussian bureaucracy as one in which the power of the crown *vis-à-vis* an increasingly confident, independent and self-important bureaucratic elite diminished. Stern service codes were indeed enforced, but growth in the

25 Cited in Herman Finer, *Theory and Practice of Modern Government*, London, 1961, p. 753, and also in E. N. Gladden, op. cit., vol. II, p. 162.
26 Krygier, 'State and Bureaucracy', p. 7.

numbers of civil servants made monocratic authority in the style of Frederick William I increasingly impossible. Hans Rosenberg writes of a sharp decline in loyalty, efficiency and service morale during the 'time of troubles' of the Seven Years' War and the subsequent economic depression that brought about the 1770 reforms, but resulted in a higher administrative service that was self-recruiting and identified with aristocratic valuations and interest.[27] Krygier emphasizes that there was nevertheless important advance toward modern 'rational' bureaucracy through the institution of the examination system, through the weakening of the collegial system by new specialist, functionally based ministries and through the increasing 'disengagement' of public officialdom from the king or dynasty.[28]

The Prussian *Allgemeines Landrecht* (General Legal Code) of 1794, drafted while Frederick was alive, brings out the 'modernizing' strain in Frederick's mentality and reign, the strength of official demands against arbitrary royal intervention and the extent to which Prussia still had to respect feudal and territorial rights. The Code 'depersonalized' government. Officials – now called 'state servants' and 'professional officials of the state' – received a qualified legal right to permanent tenure and an unqualified right to due process of law in respect of questionable conduct. The Code, as John Gillis puts it,[29] recognized them 'as a privileged corporation, subject to its own separate jurisdiction, distinct in title and rank, and exempt from many of the ordinary civil obligations'. The Code, in this respect and others, was still the Code of a *Standesstaat*, of a system having to bow to feudal ranks and territorial 'rights'.

Enlightenment principles had greater impact on the organization and role of the bureaucracy during the Napoleonic wars – especially after Prussia reeled from its defeat at Jena. The reform era was comparatively brief. The impetus slackened with the fall of Napoleon. Still, the *Kabinettsystem* was replaced by a more coherent structure of administration based on departmental responsibility to a single minister, functional rather than territorial principles of division, and a more systematic definition of

27   Rosenberg, op. cit., p. 181.
28   Krygier, 'State and Bureaucracy', pp. 6–8.
29   John R. Gillis, *The Prussian Bureaucracy in Crisis 1840–60: Origins of an Administrative Ethos*, Stanford, Ca., 1971, p. 23, as cited in Krygier, 'State and Bureaucracy', p. 8.

relationships between central ministries and provincial judicial and administrative bodies. Much jumble and confusion was cleared away, though the surviving emphasis on 'feudal' ranks and titles seemed increasingly out of step with 'modernity' as German liberal intellectuals again looked to post-Bourbon France as the rational, enlightened, unmedieval state. Increasingly, as the nineteenth century went on, there were two Germanies. There was conservative, loyal, obedient Germany looking to the Hohenzollern and beyond them to the Hohenstaufen *Reich*, to Prussia and its *Junkers*, to civil administration carried out with military precision and dedication. There was liberal Germany, looking south and west, anti-militarist, suspicious of centralization, of the *Reich* and Prussia, wanting to be neither a frontier state nor a *Reich*, but a liberal, European polity not centred upon the power of the state.

Peter the Great and Russia

The emergence of Russia as a world power was as remarkable as that of Prussia. It, too, was based on the militarization of society and government – on the building of a powerful state and army and the attempted pervasive regulation of social and political life for largely military purposes. But no Prussian king and no Prussian state ever achieved or even dreamt of the autocratic power and the universal subservience demanded by the Tsar of All the Russias, on whom all classes and institutions, favour and initiative depended. For many, Russia before and after the Revolution has stood outside 'western' society and 'western' civilization. The Russian state, unlike that of Poland and Hungary, let alone the states of western Europe, has always proved stronger than all the rest of society. All position, opportunity and innovation flowed from the top. Muscovy or the Tatars had successfully destroyed and incorporated the domains of all its rivals – Kiev, Novgorod, Suzdal', Tver' etc. – and all political pluralism with them. It was never confronted by those internal forces that produced the Reception of Roman Law, the Renaissance and humanism, or the Protestant Reformation, the growth of science and the Age of Reason.

Scholars have long discussed and continue to discuss whether this is true and, if so, why it is true. It is commonly accepted that Russia knew no true pluralizing feudalism of the European kind, with competing power centres, at least since the destruction of the boyars between the fifteenth and the eighteenth centuries, but possibly from its early beginnings under the Norse rule. Some ascribe the overwhelming powers and ambition of the state as an instrument of autocracy to the Tatar yoke and the influence of Mongol and Chinese statecraft. Others stress the Byzantine–Turkish model of Caesaro-Papism in which church and state combine to rule, or in which the church is totally subordinated to the state. The difference between neo-Platonist eastern Christianity and the Aristotelianism of the western Church has also been thought significant. Others again have emphasized Russia's lack of natural boundaries and defences, the constant threat from Livonian Knights, Lithuanian monarchs, Poles and Swedes in the west, Tatars and a succession of central Asian kingdoms and tribes in the east and south. Richard Pipes, in an important work,[30] argues that Russia's economic conditions and external situation required her to organize militarily and therefore politically in a highly efficient manner, while her climate, her poor roads and great distances, and her economy generally inhibited such organization. The state, he says, did not grow out of society nor was it imposed upon society externally. It developed rather out of princely power over their private domains. The prince's authority spread – not without meeting massive resistance – to the free population outside these domains. Russia became a 'patrimonial state' in which the lines separating ownership from sovereignty were weak or non-existent, in which private property was not seen as a realm over which public authority normally exercised no jurisdiction. Property was rather a true patrimonium – of the prince. The prince and the Tsar *owned* his kingdom. In Russia, Pipes argues, the separation between sovereignty and authority exercised as ownership occurred very late and very imperfectly: the ruler was both the sovereign of the realm and its proprietor. No social class – the peasantry, *dvorianstvo* (the serving nobility that replaced the boyars) or the 'missing bourgeoisie' – was strong enough to challenge the state. Deprived of a base in the power of property, Russian opposition to the autocracy became almost entirely intellectual, elevating ideas and thus

30 Richard Pipes, *Russia Under the Old Regime,* London, 1974, passim.

encouraging the further extension of attempted ideological control by the state.

Of course, there were bitter and colourful battles between the princes and power shifted from one city to another. They ended in the ascendancy of Moscow which had sided with the Mongol Tatars during a Russian rebellion led by the Prince of Tver'. The Mongols in 1327 conferred the title of Great Prince on Ivan Danilovich, Prince of Moscow, nicknamed *Kalita* (moneybags) and later known as Ivan I, who was the leader of the combined Mongol–Russian punitive force that devastated Tver'. They made him Farmer-General of the Tribute throughout Russia. It was an expensive privilege, as Pipes says, since it made Ivan responsible for arrears and default. But it gave Ivan a unique opportunity for meddling in the internal affairs of rival Russian princedoms and launched Moscow on its rise to pre-eminence and ultimate control.

From the fourteenth and fifteenth centuries, the Muscovite state expanded in a truly spectacular manner – from 20,000 square kilometres in 1300 to 2.8 million square kilometres in 1533 and 5.4 million square kilometres in 1600. Its rulers sought means of administering their new domains, which continued to grow at the rate of 35,000 square kilometres a year.

They appointed territorial officials – *namestniki* for the cities and *volosteli* for the rural areas (later fused and called *voevody*) – to govern the subject populations, to extract revenue for the prince and to maintain law and order. These officials carried out broad peace-keeping and military operations, commanding troops. They acted as judges in civil and criminal cases and oversaw the work of the local courts. Originally, they received no salary but were allowed and expected to feed themselves at the expense of the districts they governed by keeping some court fees and extracting payments in kind. They were difficult to control because of the vast distances that separated them from the capital and their rule was often highly exploitative. Yet it was limited in the contribution it could make to the betterment of local conditions by inactivity, or other preoccupations, at a centre long noted for the viciousness of its intrigues and the brutality and instability of many of its rulers.

By the end of the sixteenth century, the Russian monarchy had imposed compulsory service on all landowners – that is, tenure became conditional on service. Pedigreed families and clans provided the Muscovite service class but themselves controlled a complex order of precedence and set up special committees to adjudicate disputes. Allodial land holding and patrimonial nests of old families were gradually eliminated and replaced by service land. Ivan the Terrible especially and others had formed particular corps – in his case the *Oprichniki* – who acted as police, thugs, executioners and spies working against the Tsar's real or fancied enemies. By 1651, with an estimated population of 13 million, Russia had 39,000 servitors or one for every 333 inhabitants (0.3 per cent of the population).[31] There were by then two separate groups of state servitors: one group based on noble birth, the other on skill and experience. This latter group, the *prikaznye liudi*, or chancellery men, worked twelve hours a day until 1680. They were given systematic in-service training and made to specialize by geographical area and by kind of work.

In the second half of the seventeenth century, Russia implicitly recognized herself to be a 'backward country', different from advancing western Europe in its traditions, habits and social and political organization, lagging especially in effective military power while seriously threatened from without. Christian, geographically close and sensitive to western influence and aggression, it underwent a crisis of self-confidence. This was followed by a process of internal reform with which the name of Peter I (the Great) is especially associated. Born in 1672, he was crowned at the age of ten and reigned as autocrat from 1694 to 1725. Peter 'hacked a window through to Europe' by founding St Petersburg as the new capital, embarked on an ambitious policy of 'westernization' or 'Europeanization', launched Russia's first newspaper and reorganized her manners, customs and administration. He had prepared for his rule by travelling incognito to the west to work and study its political, military and technical progress with special emphasis on shipbuilding and gunnery. He modelled his court on Versailles, made western dress compulsory for his courtiers and forcibly shaved the beards of the boyars. His real interest, however, was not in westernization but in power. His measures to westernize Russia were characteristically monocratic. He did, as Pipes stresses, articulate some western seventeenth-century conceptions of the common good, general welfare

31   Ibid., p. 97.

and the benefit of the whole nation; he was genuinely concerned to bring private behaviour, the lot of ordinary people and the work of the state into accord. He made merit a formal basis of preferment in the public service by introducing a Table of Fourteen Ranks, matching civil and military positions.

All officials were required to work their way up the ranks, and all officials from the eighth rank upward to the first, regardless of origin, were ennobled. By the middle of the eighteenth century the ratio of officials of noble origin holding positions within the Table of Ranks to those of non-noble origin was virtually one-to-one, though in the top five ranks the proportion of the noble-born was 88 per cent. Basically, however, *dvorianstvo* or nobility came to signify a form of employment, a post or eligibility for a post and landholding on that basis, rather than an independent social standing. (From the 39,000 *dvoriane* in 1651, the number rose to 108,000 in 1782 and 464,000 in 1858.)[32] At the same time, however, Peter, a giant of a man with great personal courage who took part in all the major engagements of his twenty-one-year war with Sweden and personally led his armies against Turkey and Persia, was never one to flinch from the use of force, of brutal force, where he deemed it necessary. He created – at first secretly – a separate police bureau, the *Preobrazhenskii Prikaz*, charged with overall responsiblity for dealing with political offences in the Empire and free to investigate at the discretion of its head any institution and any individual regardless of rank. Not even the Imperial Senate which Peter had set up to supervise the country's administration had the right to inquire into its affairs. Thousands, Pipes reminds us, were tortured and put to death in its chambers. It was this organ which was ultimately called in to manage the construction of St Petersburg, bogged down in various unsuccessful attempts.

The more general administrative reforms initiated by Peter were meant to make government officers involve themselves actively in the expansion of trade and commerce, the maintenance of food and supplies, the upkeep of roads, the proper ordering of factories, the education and moral development of the population. Initially, between 1707 and 1710, Peter had divided Russia into ten huge provinces or *gubernii* ruled by a strong vice-regal provincial chief enjoying the Tsar's personal favour. At

32   Ibid., p. 131, drawing on the Soviet historians V.M. Kabuzan and S.M. Troitskii.

that stage he seemed to favour the deconcentration of power and to be influenced by German administrative models. In 1714 he issued a decree calling on the local gentry to elect councillors (*landraty*) to advise the governors. The law stipulated that when his councillors met, the governor was to preside, but he was to do so as a president not a ruler. By 1719, Peter had become disenchanted with his attempts at decentralization and with his governors. The central administration was strengthened. Many of the functions of the *gubernii* and their governors were transfered to the Imperial Senate and the Colleges in St Petersburg. The *gubernii* were sub-divided into *provintsii*. These became important administrative districts, but were required to share authority with a variety of independent agencies – representatives of the central colleges, local military commanders and the courts. The Empire, however, as R.G. Robbins writes, lacked the financial and human resources necessary to support the large network of offices and officials Peter had envisaged, while the underdevelopment of the nation's social classes doomed the experiments in self-government. One of Peter's most significant introductions, however, was the office of Procurator General established in 1722. This official watched over the working of the colleges through his own procurators, took over the whole staff of the Fiscal and acted as president of the Senate when Peter was not present. In the latter part of his reign, however, Peter, restless as ever, again became dissatisfied with the instruments of control he had created. He fell into the habit of using his trusted guards officers, brought up at court, employed as a sort of janissary force and completely loyal to Peter They had been used originally to compel other troops to discipline; now, Peter gave them overriding commissions to enforce similar 'discipline' in the various government institutions.[33]

On Peter's death in 1725, Robbins concludes, Russian provincial administration was a tangled mess. One significant legacy, apart from the procuracy, remained: an activist style of local government and a provincial chief with wide powers derived from his personal connection with the autocrat. Not until the

33 I draw here on Richard G. Robbins, Jr., *The Tsar's Viceroys: Russian Provincial Governors in the Last Years of the Empire*, Ithaca and London, 1987, pp. 5–8, and more generally, *passim*; on Walter McKenzie Pintner and Don Karl Rowney, eds, *Russian Officialdom: The Bureaucratization of Russian Society from the Seventeenth to the Twentieth Century*, London, 1980, on Pipes, op. cit., and on Tibor Szamuely, *The Russian Tradition*, London, 1974.

reforms initiated by Catherine the Great between 1775 and 1785 did Russia have a comparatively regularized system of administration which sought to combine personal autocracy, regular institutions and procedures, and class self-government in a decentralized setting. Catherine, though too often remembered for her love affairs, was the one who revolutionized the Russian administrative system and set it on a more western course. In 1762 Peter III had issued a manifesto exempting Russian *dvoriane* from state service; Catherine confirmed this and other liberties acquired by the *dvorianstvo* since the death of Peter the Great, recognized the land they held as their legal property and exempted them from corporal punishment. From then on, *dvoriane* came to be more like western landowners, while servitors with governmental posts came to be called *chinovniki* (holders of rank). Earlier, Catherine had departed from Peter the Great's insistence on merit by ordering automatic promotions for high civil servants who had held the post for seven (later three) years. The result was that the monarch continued to enjoy unlimited authority in the sphere of foreign policy and in disposing at pleasure of that part of the revenue which actually reached the treasury. In governing the country, however, as Pipes stresses, 'he was severely constrained by the power of his one-time servitors – dvoriane and chinovniki.'[34] A Russian historian has indeed argued that after Catherine Russia could be divided into two parts – the twenty-eight provinces concentrated in the geographical centre of the country, which were the heartland of serfdom, and where the *dvoriane* ruled, and the more peripheral parts where the bureaucrat took over. After 1762, Pipes concludes, 'the Russian monarchy became in large measure the captive of groups which it had originally brought into existence. The trappings of imperial omnipotence served merely to conceal its desperate weakness – as well as to camouflage the actual power wielded by the dvoriane and chinovniki.'[35] Only the weakness of the traditional social groupings prevented any of them from seizing the political prerogatives claimed by the crown until the authority of the state itself collapsed under the stresses of the First World War.

Catherine had set up such new institutions as the provincial

34 Pipes, op. cit., p. 137.
35 Ibid., p. 138.

boards, the fiscal chamber, the welfare board, and new judicial bodies charged with seeing that laws were understood and obeyed. For the first time, the Russian Empire now had a comprehensive network of provincial institutions as part of a unified territorial administration, though their powers were not well defined. In the eighteenth century, they were on the whole unchecked by the intrusion of central officers or by local institutions of self-government; with the creation of ministries in 1802 government became somewhat less personal and more regularized. Alexander I's principal adviser, the active Russian political and administrative reformer Count Michael Speransky, in 1802 denounced Russian backwardness and corruption; in 1809 he submitted to the Tsar his *Introduction to the Constitution of the Laws of State*. His aim was to replace the arbitrary autocracy with an absolute monarchy recognizing a *Rechtsstaat*, based on a firm legal framework and an efficient bureaucracy. He separated the legislative, judicial and administrative functions of government and divided society into three 'estates': the nobility, the middle class and the peasantry. (Clearly opposed to serfdom – finally abolished under Alexander II, in 1861 – Speransky thought emancipation would have to be accomplished slowly and be preceded by a long process of education.) Immediately, the estates should have equality before the law and civil rights according to their status; there should be an independent judiciary and coordinated ministries should be answerable, through their ministers, to a (consultative) State *Duma* at the head of a four-tier system of noble-elected assemblies. The State *Duma*, though on a broader electoral base and with limited and vetoable control of the budget, was not established until after the 1905 revolution, in 1906, and dissolved within a few months. Three more were to meet between 1907 and 1917. In Speransky's time, the provincial governors came under the increasing control of the Ministry of Internal Affairs, but they still remained in many respects viceroys, creatures of the emperor and linked to him directly. Speransky's *Introduction* achieved little until Alexander II's reforms from above in 1861–66. Until 1917, indeed, as Robbins says, the centre continued to vacillate between seeing the governorship as an organ of supervision with a sharply limited sphere of operation and strengthening gubernatorial power in the interests of preventing direct or indirect challenges to the autocracy. The administration of *gubernii* remained fragmented, challenged by self-government and local representatives of St Petersburg ministries and crumbling before the Herculean proportions of the tasks expected of the governor. At the centre, things were not much better: *Chinovnichestvo* (bureaucracy and bureaucratic behaviour) had, justifiably, a far worse press in the Russian Empire than in western Europe. It was renowned neither for its dedication nor for its efficiency – though there were able men and efficient departments (among which the secret police ranked high).

Austria

The most surprising thing about the Austro-Hungarian Empire, Karl Kautsky once said, was not its collapse in 1918, but its survival until then. The Habsburg Holy Roman Empire, officially ruled from Vienna until 1806, had not been strong enough to establish an effective centralized power in Germany, though the influence of the imperial courts on the development of public law in Germany should not be underrated. The German territorial princes ruled in societies organized, as Prussia had been, on the principle of patrimonial estates. They held bundles of acquired rights derived from a variety of sources and positions, formally acknowledged the overlordship of the Emperor, and were often confronted by their subjects or other bodies with acquired rights of equal force. The imperial courts from the end of the fifteenth century exercised jurisdiction in such conflict between princes and their subjects and did so significantly until a new conception of the prince as having a general and largely overriding police power (*ius politiae*) to protect the welfare and security of his subjects was successfully asserted as part of the princely struggle for independence. That power was held to take precedence over private individual interests and to put authoritative 'police' regulations – that is, government administration (*Regierung*) – outside private law and therefore outside the power of the imperial court to intervene. A clearer separation between the person of the prince and his public function as prince resulted. It was accompanied, in an endeavour to give some judicial redress against administrative acts of the prince, by the new theory of the *fiscus*. The idea was that the public patrimony and the public treasury were not the personal property of the prince, but were held by a legal personality, the *fiscus* – analogous in this respect to the modern concept of the crown. The *fiscus* as holder of property, however, could be sued for compensation in private law – for wrongfully seizing property without compensation, or depriving a subject of an office to which the subject was entitled. Well into the nineteenth century, Germany used the private law concept of the *fiscus* and the public law concept of 'police power' to regulate what in France after Napoleon had been taken right out of the ordinary system of courts and subjected to a special administrative system of appeal headed by a *Conseil d'Etat*. In Austria itself, important administrative innovations and reforms – recruitment on merit, professional training, centralization – were introduced by the enlightened monarchs Maria Theresa (r. 1740–50) and Joseph II (co-regent and Emperor 1765–90).

England

England, by the end of the eighteenth century, had perhaps done least to 'rationalize' its system of administration, which continued to betray both its medieval origins and the pluralism and independence, the anti-administrative character, of the Common Law. At the local level, Paul Finn reminds us, service in offices was both compulsory and unpaid. At the central level, it was generally still a matter of patronage. Rewards – related to the office but not to the work done, if it was done at all – came from salary or from fees paid by members of the public or from poundage on money receipts or from usufruct of moneys in an officer's hand or from customary perquisites and gratuities. Offices were still regarded as a form of property. They were incorporeal hereditaments, which could be granted to a person and his heirs, or for life, or for a term of years, or during pleasure only. Sinecures abounded. In late eighteenth-century England, Finn concludes,

> Customs, Excise and the Post Office apart, the central civil administration was a small affair indeed, bearing little on the everyday life of ordinary citizens. Not even the great officers of state

– the Principal Secretaries, the Lord Treasurer and the like – were possessed of significant common law or statutory functions. They did not 'have any very important share of magistracy conferred upon them' and were not 'in any considerable degree the objects of our laws'. Such central public agencies as there were, were randomly organized, unco-ordinated, largely unsupervised, burdened with sinecures and affected by some corruption. For their waste and inefficiencies they were the objects of recurrent criticisms. The strictures of the great jurist Sir Matthew Hale, published in 1787 but written a century earlier, are eloquent on the enduring administrative malaise: 'There are at this day in the exchequer many great officers that receive the profit and fees of their office, and either do not at all attend it, or know not what belongs to it, but only perchance once a term sit with some formality in their gowns, but never put their hands to any business of their offices, nor indeed know not how'. The practical governance of the country was effected through local, not national, officials and agencies; in particular through the justices of the peace, vestries and parish officers, and special-purpose statutory commissions and trusts. They were entrusted with much of the implementation and enforcement of legislation and with the maintenance of public order. The justices held office from the King at pleasure; the great majority were, for practical purposes, unpaid and were drawn from the landed class and from the clergy. While treated with little tenderness by courts not slow to countenance claims of irregularities, the justices themselves were free from, and resistant to, control from the central government. From late medieval times, and in and out of sessions, they had been entrusted with an ever-widening array of functions. In addition to their criminal jurisdiction, the poor law, policing, public works, roads, the regulation of labour and commerce, licensing, vagrancy, gaols and houses of correction fell, at one time or another, into their ken. Their activities, as also those of the vestries and of the borough corporations, were supplemented progressively by an ever-growing number of statutory boards. These were charged mainly with the erection and maintenance of public works and utilities and with the provision of amenity services – roads, turnpikes, paving, lighting, drainage, waterways, ports and harbours and the like. Of particular importance from the latter part of the eighteenth century were the many improvement trusts for [the] amelioration of conditions in the rapidly-growing urban districts. [36]

36 Paul D. Finn, *Law and Government in Colonial Australia*, Melbourne, 1987, p. 8.

It is common to see the Northcote–Trevelyan reforms of the 1850s, commissioned partly in response to the 1848 revolutions in Europe and displaying the administrative experience gained by the East India Company in supervising, employing or advising administrators in a huge sub-continent, as inaugurating 'modern' public administration in England, to be discussed in the next chapter. L.J. Hume, on the other hand, in his *Bentham and Bureaucracy* (Cambridge, 1981) has stressed Britain's early achievement of legal unity and centralization, the relative unimportance of 'venality' in appointments to office and the relatively early sloughing off of 'farming' in taxation and the relatively effective control of local authorities. He has contrasted this with the continental monarchies, whose claims were repeatedly frustrated or falsified by nobles, the church, provincial courts and estates and recalcitrant officials, as well as by financiers whom the state could neither discipline nor do without.

Yet, the English Common Law as one not deriving all authority from the state, the institution of the trust and the use of statutory boards and commissions all helped to produce in England a genuine alternative to the strongly hierarchical and rigidly centrally directed 'ideal rational bureaucracies' aimed at by the French or the disciplined and efficient carrying out of Imperial will and national goals aimed at by at least some of the rulers of Prussia and Russia and some of their servants.

4

Capitalism, Socialism and Bureaucracy

From Enlightenment to democracy

By the end of the eighteenth century systematic concern with the
theory and practice of regularized administration as a central
function of government was burgeoning throughout Europe.
Growth in population, production and trade, the conversion of
wars from dynastic into national wars, the acquisition of colonies,
the foundation and expansion of great capital cities, all played a
role. So did the increasing social importance of the literate middle
classes and the decline of an aristocracy deriving its claim to
authority from origin and military conquests. Above all, however, the Enlightenment, and its heirs in England, the philosophical radicals, were introducing, or strengthening, demands
that governments *perform*, that they improve the position of
their people and the public welfare, that they convert royal
servants into public servants, the crown into the state, office into
a public trust. The Industrial Revolution and the growth of
scientific knowledge intensified these developments and added
yet other dimensions. These were a much more advanced
division of labour, increasing need and respect for specialization
and technical knowledge (both in the broad and in the narrow
sense of 'technical') and a much more urgent sense of economic
development, public health and human progress, to which
government and administration might and should make a significant contribution. As the nineteenth century progressed, the
accelerated building of public roads and facilities, the introduction of gas, electricity and the telephone all required corps of
officials with a degree of training. So did the introduction of
military conscription and of new scientific and technological
services for modern armies, and then navies. Education, ecclesiastical affairs, and cultural agencies, like the institutions of
commerce, industry and agriculture, new or greatly enlarged,

required similar services. The increasing social problems connected with modern industry – factory inspection, legislation for working conditions, poor relief, workers' compensation and insurance, public housing, public health and other services – all called for administrative personnel on a large scale. Laws affecting these matters increasingly required skills and knowledge beyond the capacities of local amateurs, whether elected or voluntary. The industrial technology itself and later a host of scientific technologies, having extended enormously the harm that human actions and possessions might do to others, provoked – partly through outrage over individual mishaps or abuses – more and more government action, inspection and control. All this encouraged governments to perform new functions and made possible and necessary the employment of many more civil servants on the basis of ever-increasing revenue through taxation. Even in the eighteenth century, theorists of 'police' (the polity) and of political economy had emphasized the role of centrally made and directed laws, capable of clarification, improvement and organization into a coherent body of rational law. The shift, as Leonard Krieger has put it, was from an authority of origins to an authority of ends. An influential metaphor was that of government as an administrative machine – favoured especially in the periods or in the countries where the ruler could plausibly and flatteringly be presented as the foreman, the mainspring, the operator, who sets everything in motion. Subsequent writers on bureaucracy and the Enlightenment have reminded us of striking contemporary quotations:

A properly constituted state must be exactly analogous to a machine, in which all the wheels and gears are precisely adjusted to one another; and the ruler must be the foreman, the mainspring, or the soul – if one may use the expression – which sets everything in motion.[1]

Just as radii starting from different points on a circumference converge all at a common center, so all the parts of the administration

1 J.H.G. von Justi, *Gesammelte Politische- und Finanzschriften*, Copenhagen and Leipzig, 1761, vol. III, pp. 86–7, as translated in Geraint Parry, 'Enlightened Government and its Critics in Eighteenth-Century Germany', in *Historical Journal*, vol. VI, 1963, pp. 178–92 at p. 184; see also Leonard Krieger, *An Essay on the Theory of Enlightened Despotism*, Chicago, 1975, p. 40.

are mutually interlocked and must converge to the same goal. If, therefore, the movement of the individual parts is not calculated in terms of this general rule, the general result can only be an incoherence which will hamper their regular performance.

To avoid this defect, those who are entrusted with the task of renovating the shapeless edifice of our social contract according to correct principles must know the structure of the whole machine; and by constantly keeping in view its movement, they shall be in a better position to see the defects of its wheels and gears. This will enable them to have a better grasp of what improvements are required.[2]

In eighteenth-century France, as a modern scholar has put it:

the word 'machine' has been increasingly used to describe adminis-trative organizations. By the end of the eighteenth century the machine had become an obsessive image. Anson used it to describe the projected Ministry of the Interior, Camus to describe the entire administration, Marat to represent municipal administrations, and to sum up, the machine image in the writings of Lebrun, Roederer, Laffon de Ladébat and many others seems to show that this generation thought of administrative and political agencies as analogous to machines. The other possible analogy, comparing the organization to the human body as Hobbes for instance had done, seldom appears in the writings of the late eighteenth-century French reformers and revolutionaries.[3]

Machines, as Bosher goes on, have a function. In France, the posts occupied by officials during the *ancien régime* had been offices, charges or places. Soon after the Revolution, they came to be called *emplois* or *fonctions* and the officials themselves *fonctionnaires*.

The French Revolution stood for the consummation of the Enlightenment. It saw government and administration as need-ing to be based on principles of rationality, welfare and utility.

2 Quoted, from 'The Principles of Government Reform' drafted in 1802 by the 'Unofficial Committee' set up in St Petersburg by Alexander I, in Marc Raeff, *Plans for Political Reform in Imperial Russia, 1730–1905*, Englewood Cliffs, NJ, 1966, p. 89, and cited in Martin Krygier, 'State and Bureaucracy in Europe: The Growth of a Concept', in Kamenka and Krygier, eds, *Bureaucracy – The Career of a Concept*, London, 1979, pp. 1–33 at p. 17.

3 J.F. Bosher, *French Finances 1770–1795: From Business to Bureaucracy*, Cam-bridge, 1970, p. 296; cited by Krygier, 'State and Bureaucracy', p. 17.

But it also saw government and its officials as servants of the people. It rejected, at least in principle, the notion that the *fonctionnaire* was part of a caste or class having a special standing in society by virtue of being an office-holder. In principle, bureaucrats were being robbed of their special standing as part of a ranked society or as an extension of royal power and prestige. The bureaucracy was being transformed into a civil service.

On the continent, the emphasis was on creating or reforming a total administrative system as part of the political direction of the society from the top. This paralleled the Enlightenment and continental Civil Law conception of legal regulation as requiring the elaboration of general principles and systematic codes which would then be applied to specific cases. In English politics, administration and law, the tendency was the opposite – to work toward more general principles and structures from specific problems, cases and needs, to work from the particular to the general and not vice versa. A.V. Dicey in his classic *Lectures on Law and Opinion in the Nineteenth Century* (first published in 1905) sought to account for the massive growth of state intervention in Britain as the nineteenth century progressed by relating legislation and even the absence of legislation to the varying currents of public opinion. The story as he told it was a persuasive and subtle one. It put much weight on the influence of Jeremy Bentham and the philosophical radicals, the debates on the Poor Law and the fear of Chartism. It distinguished the 'Old Toryism' with its mercantilist economists and the associated landed gentry from an ethos of individualism and *laissez-faire* and both in turn from the new 'collectivism' threatening, as Dicey saw it, to dominate the twentieth century. Against this, we have had the attack on Dicey launched, fifty years later, by Oliver MacDonagh, in his seminal article 'Delegated Legislation and Administrative Discretions in the 1850s: A Particular Study', published in *Victorian Studies* in 1958 (vol. 2, pp. 29–44). This was followed up and incorporated in his *A Pattern of Government Growth 1800–1860: The Passenger Acts and Their Enforcement* (London, 1961). MacDonagh's reappraisal of Dicey had him arguing that outrage over specific abuses provided a much more powerful impetus toward government intervention and administrative reform than philosophical radicalism and that it did so successfully in the very heyday of *laissez-faire* individualism and emphasis on the freedom of contract. He showed this convincingly first in his earlier work on emigration and the Passenger Acts and then went on to see the same mechanism at work in mines and factories, in shipping and public health. As Roy MacLeod, summarizing MacDonagh's impact on the study of administration in England, puts it, MacDonagh provided a new 'model' which described five stages in the response of Victorian government to the 'social evils' Britain encountered between 1825 and 1870:

> The first stage consisted in the exposure of the 'evil' itself, a disaster, or an outrage – for example, an explosion in the coal fields, the arrival of cholera – in short, an 'intolerable situation'. In response, Parliament typically passed initial, permissive or enabling legislation; but without means of enforcement, short of appeal to the courts, this proved inadequate. When experience of the 'evil' continued, a second stage ensued, in which special officers, inspectors and other 'experts' were appointed to enforce the new legislation. As these officers responded to the continuing needs of their clients and their consciences, they pressed for further compulsory legislation, and for a superintending central body to oversee it, reporting regularly, but at several removes, to Parliament. In many cases, this still failed to go far enough, and a fourth stage ensued, in which the experts ceased to regard the problems they faced as soluble simply by more legislation and additional staff. They sought to apply their expertise, extending government into areas it had not contemplated entering. Their realism ultimately gave way to a fifth stage, in which officers took upon themselves a wider ambit of administrative discretion. Their 'more or less conscious Fabianism' extended their use of new scientific knowledge to prevent rather than merely cure the evils they confronted. This gave a 'dynamic role for government within society'. In the process, a 'new sort of state was being born'.[4]

MacDonagh's work produced both considerable debate and what MacLeod calls 'a "paradigm shift" in the historiography of Victorian government'.[5] Others have examined and re-examined some of his and Dicey's conceptual terms, but they have also studied in detail individual government departments

4 Roy MacLeod, 'Introduction', in Roy MacLeod, ed., *Government and Expertise: Specialists, Administrators and Professionals, 1860–1919*, Cambridge, 1988, p. 4.
5 Ibid., p. 5.

(the Education Department, the Board of Trade and the Local Government Board) and such agencies of enquiry as Royal Commissions and Select Committees. MacDonagh himself, in *Early Victorian Government, 1830–1870* (London, 1977), modified a little his anti-ideological stance and described the forces assisting government growth as theoretical, political and technical – that is ideology, including the Benthamite, popular outrage and demand and the growth of expertise. Roy MacLeod, in another context, has argued that the wider reform movement of which the demand for administrative reform was part, represented the gradual advance not of any radical politics, but of the Peelite tradition of change combined with accommodation, effectively incorporated in Gladstone's liberalism.[6]

Historians of the growth of administrative government in Britain, MacLeod reminds us, now customarily follow Dicey in describing that growth as passing, in the nineteenth century, through three phases. The first phase, from the end of the Napoleonic Wars in 1815 to the Reform Act of 1832, was a period of 'legislative quiescence', of 'Old Toryism', which saw government prepared to act primarily 'against the injustices of agricultural distress, and the pressures of overpopulation, crime and the miseries of city life'. In the second phase, from the 1830s to the late 1860s, 'scientists and social scientists, Benthamites and Utilitarians, clergymen and "calculators" of the statistical movement, joined with Parliamentary crusaders to deploy the rhetoric of improvement and reform'. For by then, 'a new humanism', drawing on the Benthamites and the Evangelicals, had made social evils seem intolerable. It is in this period, the 'heyday' of *laissez-faire*, that we see the now familiar explosion of government intervention of which MacDonagh and others have written and recommendations for Civil Service reform. The third phase – from 1870 to 1900 – sees the Civil Service indeed reformed and ends with it becoming the pride of Britain and Empire.[7]

6   Roy M. MacLeod, 'Whigs and Savants: Reflections on the Reform Movement in the Royal Society, 1830–48', in Ian Inkster and Jack Morrell, eds, *Metropolis and Province: Science in British Culture, 1780–1850*, London, 1983, pp. 55–90, as cited in Nicolaas A. Rupke, 'The Road to Albertopolis: Richard Owen (1804–92) and the Founding of the British Museum of Natural History', in N.A. Rupke, ed., *Science, Politics and the Public Good: Essays in Honour of Margaret Gowing*, London, 1988, pp. 63–89 at p. 78.
7   MacLeod, *Government and Expertise*, p. 9.

The nineteenth century, then, saw both the growth of industrial society, with its attendant evils and its increasing elevation and provision of expertise, and the growth of and increasing demand for democracy and the righting of social evils. Characteristic of the Victorian revolution in government, another historian reminds us,

> was the acceptance of public responsibility for a great many social problems which only experts could solve. Such problems, which were felt most acutely by local governments, included building tramways, new streets, bridges, libraries, town halls, plants and distribution systems for gas and later for electricity, as well as obtaining water supplies and building sewerage systems.[8]

Democracy, it was soon realized, could not really mean executive government by the people in any society whose citizens could not be assembled in the town square. Nor could the people directly provide the now needed expertise for righting or avoiding the new social evils. Democracy for the majority of the nineteenth- and twentieth-century theorists meant the accountability of government and of its officials to the people or their representatives through regular elections and the reservation of policy-making powers to Parliament itself. The main developments in public administration in the nineteenth century lay in the direction of combating what were thought of as aristocratic hangovers – advantages of birth or connections, patronage and sinecures and the corruption associated with this. These were now seen as inimical to democracy, to the efficient and technically competent care for the health and safety, the economic and political welfare, of citizens, and to honest government. In 1853, the British Prime Minister, Lord Aberdeen, called upon Sir Stafford Northcote, a politician, and Sir Charles Edward Trevelyan, senior permanent official at Her Majesty's Treasury, who had begun serving in the East India Company as a writer at the age of nineteen, to formulate a scheme to reorganize the Civil Service. The Northcote–Trevelyan Report completed at the end of that

8 Christopher Hamlin, 'Politics and Germ Theories in Victorian Britain: The Metropolitan Water Commissions of 1867–9 and 1892–3', in MacLeod, op. cit., pp. 110–27 at pp. 110–11.

year and embodied in an official state document was to have –
delayed – revolutionary influence upon the British Civil Service
and through it upon many public services throughout the world.
It recommended the abolition of patronage and drew upon
Chinese practice to urge recruitment by open competitive examinations under the supervision of a central examining board. It
proposed the reorganization of the office staff of the central
departments into two broad classes – one to deal with intellectual
work, the other with mechanical. It recommended the filling of
higher posts by promotion from inside the service on the basis of
merit rather than seniority. On the intellectual side it elevated
'generalist' against technical education. The Report, of course,
led to much controversy. The principle of open competition in
recruitment was not adopted until 1870 – but after 1855
appointees had to submit themselves to a pass examination even
though they were still nominated by heads of departments. Some
departments began to introduce open competition on their own
account. Public pressure for reform grew with the revelation of
organizational shortcomings in the several war departments
during the Crimean War, just as it had grown during the second
Anglo-Dutch War of 1665–67 leading parliament then to
appoint Commissioners of Public Accounts to examine Charles
II's administration, especially in regard to seamen's pay, as it
had grown in the 1780s after England's defeat in the American
War and just as it would grow in the United States after the Civil
War.

In less traditional and non-aristocratic societies such as the
United States, the war (there still not wholly won) was against
newer but open forms of patronage and new anti-democratic
advantages: political patronage and the advantages of wealth.
The movement represented by the Northcote–Trevelyan recommendations was neatly summed up in a report prepared for
President Ulysses S. Grant by Dorman B. Eaton. In 1871
President Grant had secured Congress approval to make new
regulations for the admission of persons into the US Civil Service
and appointed an advisory committee to draw up rules for
competitive examinations. Eaton, one of the advisers, was sent
to Great Britain to report on the situation there after the implementation of the Northcote–Trevelyan proposal. Some of the

principles and conclusions Eaton derived from his study summarized neatly the nineteenth-century trend in public administration in English-speaking democracies from the United States to Australia:

1. Public office creates a relation of trust and duty of a kind which requires all authority and influence pertaining to it to be exercised with the same absolute conformity to moral standards, to the spirit of the constitution and the laws, and to the common interests of the people, which may be insisted upon in the use of public money or any other common property of the people; and, therefore, whatever difficulty may attend the practical application of the rule of duty, it is identically the same whether it be applied to property or to official discretion. There can in principle be no official discretion to disregard common interests or to grant official favors to persons or to parties.

2. So far as any right is involved, in filling offices, it is the right of the people to have the worthiest citizen in the public service for the general welfare; and the privilege of sharing the honors and profits of holding office appertains equally to every citizen in proportion to his measure of character and capacity which qualify him for such service.

4. The ability, attainments, and character requisite for the fit discharge of official duties of any kind – in other words, the personal merits of the candidate – are *in themselves the highest claim* upon an office.

5. Party government and the salutary activity of parties are not superseded, but they are made purer and more efficient, by the *merit system* of office, which brings larger capacity and higher character to their support ...

8. Examinations (in connection with investigations of character) may be so conducted as to ascertain, with far greater certainty than by any other means, the persons who are most fit for the public service; and the worthiest thus disclosed may be selected for the public service by a just and non-partisan method, which the most enlightened public opinion will heartily approve.

9. Open competition presents at once the most just and practicable means of supplying fit persons for appointment. It is proved to have given the best public servants: it makes an end of patronage; and,

besides being based on equal rights and common justice, it has been found to be the surest safeguard against both partisan coercion and official favoritism . . .

13. Open competition is as fatal to all the conditions of a beaurocracy, (sic) as it is to patronage, nepotism and every form of favoritism, in the public service.

14. The merit system, by raising the character and capacity of the subordinate service, and by accustoming the people to consider personal worth and sound principles, rather than selfish interest and adroit management, as the controlling elements of success in politics, has also invigorated national patriotism, raised the standard of statesmanship, and caused political leaders to look more to the better sentiments and the higher intelligence for support.[9]

Even in the new or reformed nineteenth- and twentieth-century democracies, the character and the spirit of government administration could vary significantly, just as the character of and respect accorded to the state could depend as much on historical tradition and social circumstance as on current political-administrative theory. Thus Englishmen from Carlyle onward were inclined to think 'bureaucracy' a continental disease and the internal administrative pretensions of the Prussian and the French states grossly excessive. Party political patronage was a special problem in America and in some other societies where it could extend down to the very lowest levels of the civil service. (The Eaton recommendations were in fact stalemated.) But in English-speaking democracies, the creation of a civil service recruited on merit and subject to parliamentary and legal checks and the scrutiny of a free press and public opinion led – at least among its supporters – to the belief that it did not deserve the unfavourable connotations of the word bureaucracy. Walter Bagehot in *The English Constitution* (1867) contrasted *bureaucracy* not backed by wider experience and opinion with *public*

9 Dorman B. Eaton, *Civil Service in Great Britain*, New York, 1880, pp. 363–6, as cited in E.N. Gladden, *A History of Public Administration*, vol. II: *From the Eleventh Century to the Present Day*, London, 1972, pp. 316–67. Eaton's numbering, which omits 3, has been followed by Gladden and here. The omission of paragraphs 6, 7, 10, 11 and 12 is mine.

administration in a parliamentary system with its frequent change of ministers – new men sensitive to outside opinion, able to reinvigorate the administrative process. For Bagehot believed that a skilled bureaucracy, trained from early life to its special vocation, lacked the flexibility necessary for meeting new problems. Similarly, Harold Laski, in the 1930 *Encyclopaedia of the Social Sciences*, defined bureaucracy as 'the term usually applied to a system of government the control of which is so completely in the hands of officials that their power jeopardizes the liberties of ordinary citizens. The characteristics of such a regime', he continued, 'are a passion for routine in administration, the sacrifice of flexibility to rule, delay in the making of decisions and a refusal to embark upon experiment. In extreme cases the members of a bureaucracy may become a hereditary caste manipulating the government to their own advantage'.[10] Democracy, Laski believed, had destroyed the old connection between bureaucracy and aristocracy as well as the corruption of previous times – 'the economic morality of the modern civil service, where it has had the advantage of permanence, has been far higher than that of private enterprise.'[11] Of course, the complex and large-scale nature of the modern state and the vastness of the services it renders made expert administration inevitable while making it almost impossible for parliament to supervise departmental action effectively and in detail. Permanence, hierarchy and professionalism, Laski insisted, were probably fundamental to the proper performance of a civil service. The inevitable tendency for such a service to degenerate into a caste with closed mind could be inhibited, but not infallibly prevented altogether. One should give the heads of departments a permanent place in public life, encourage direct and continuous contact with representative public associations, keep the retiring age of officials reasonably low and thus afford younger officials a chance of responsible work at a sufficiently early age. Decentralization would encourage action and decisiveness and greater contact with the public servant's local constituency. Changing work assignments and contact with foreign officials were important, so were not penalizing those who wished to leave the service in the early years of

10 H. Laski in *Encyclopaedia of the Social Sciences*, ed. F R.A. Seligman, vol. 3, New York, 1930, p. 70.
11 Op. cit., p. 72.

their career and creating links between elected and appointed officials, e.g. through a municipal system. Control of and protest against administrative discretion by publicity and by judicial action, e.g. a suit in tort, must be safeguarded.

Max Weber, as Martin Albrow has reminded us,[12] was also concerned with placing limitations on bureaucracy. He was not concerned with the danger of internal bureaucratic inefficiency – he believed true, ideal-type bureaucratic organization to be, above all, efficient. He worried rather about the inherent tendency of a bureaucracy to accumulate power. It had to be prevented from controlling the policy and action of the state or organization it was supposed to serve. Germany under Bismarck, he believed, had become enfeebled through the Chancellor's allowing officials to occupy desirable positions in the state. It had become a politically stultified nation in which the vigour of the non-bureaucratic classes could not express itself.

Weber considered a number of mechanisms that might limit the scope of systems of authority in general and bureaucracy in particular. Albrow has summarized them as falling into five major categories. *Collegiality*, of which there were many forms, made a number of persons responsible as of right for reaching a decision. It thus limited bureaucracy by attacking its fundamental principle: that one person and one person only had the responsibility for taking a decision at each level. Collegiality limiting one-person authority was an advantage, but the disadvantages in not reaching decisions quickly or attributing responsibility meant that it would tend to be overwhelmed by the monocratic principle.

The *separation of powers*, dividing responsibility for the same function between two or more bodies, amounted to a similar limitation of monocratic principle. It encouraged compromise between a number of interests but it could – and Weber believed it did and would – become inherently unstable, with one of the authorities gaining pre-eminence.

Amateur administration by those with sufficient resources to spend their time in unremunerated activities provided less dependence on the centre and encouraged reliance on public esteem for authority. But in modern specialized and complex societies amateurs had to be assisted by professionals and the latter tended to make the real decisions.

12   Martin Albrow, *Bureaucracy*, London, 1970, pp. 47–9.

Direct democracy sought to make officials directly guided by and answerable to an assembly through such devices as short terms of office, selection by lot and the permanent possibility of recall. As a method of administration it was feasible in small organizations or communities but even there the demand for expertise was a decisive counterweight.

Representation. In the end, Weber came to see modern parliamentary democracy as providing the greatest possibility of a check on bureaucracy. True, as Albrow emphasizes, Weber's enthusiasm for parliamentary democracy rested on his belief that the system threw up the able leaders on whom national greatness depended. He was much less concerned with democratic values. Party leaders, for him, because they came out of the increasingly bureaucratic political parties of the modern world, were not dilettantes. Their charisma was tempered by the discipline and concern for routine demanded by the modern party machine. They were therefore able to exercise real control over the state administration, to steer society, as Albrow puts it, on 'a middle course between the Scylla of mass irrationality and the Charybdis of bureaucratic tyranny'.

The two faces of capitalism

For much of the nineteenth century, the new capitalist order was seen as incorporating the reality of the demand for parliamentary democracy, legal equality for citizens, the guarantee of (individual) human rights, primarily against the state, and a defeasible (i.e. contestable) presumption against interference by the community or its actual or self-proclaimed representatives. Basically, however, capitalism was an economic concept. It was the society of free enterprise, of industrial production for a market on the basis of private ownership, freedom of contract and freedom from unnecessary state controls or gratuitous government planning. Its supporters held, as an article of faith, that individual effort and commercial enterprise were the mainsprings of progress, the source of vigour and inventiveness, the creators of wealth. Governments and their servants were essentially parasitic. Where eighteenth- and even early nineteenth-century attacks on bureaucracy emphasized its nature as a caste, its pseudo-aristocratic arrogance, its readiness to dominate, the attack shifts – as the century progresses – to the view that the power of the state is or will be at the expense of the development of citizens, of communal institutions and of individual enterprise. John Stuart Mill, in his *Principles of Political Economy*, opposed 'concentrating in a dominant bureaucracy all the skill and experience in the management of large interests, and all the power of organized action, existing in the community'.[13] In *Representative Government*, he concluded that 'the comparison ... as to the intellectual attributes of a government, has to be made between a representative democracy and a bureaucracy; all other governments may be left out of the account'. Bureaucrats are expert; they operate by well-tried and well-considered maxims and are staffed by trained people. Nevertheless, 'The disease which afflicts bureaucratic governments, and which they usually die of, is routine. They perish by the immutability of their maxims; and, still more, by the universal law that whatever becomes a routine loses its vital principle . ..'[14] In *On Liberty*, Mill had gone still further. Expanding functions of government and the greater efficiency of government would end in monop- olizing the talent of the nation – the bureaucracy would do everything and nothing could be done outside it or against its wishes. For Bagehot, the skills of a bureaucracy had only the appearance of science; they were in truth inconsistent with the proper principles of the art of business. Herbert Spencer, inexplicably but nevertheless most effectively the general and political mentor of a generation, attacked the Liberals in 1884 for espousing state intervention: 'Increasing power of a growing administrative organization is accompanied by decreasing power of the rest of society to resist its further growth and control bureaucracy. The multiplicity of careers opened by a developing bureaucracy tempts members of society to acquiesce in or favour such further growth.'[15] F.C. Montague, in *The Limits of*

13   J.S. Mill, *Principles of Political Economy*, London, 1848, vol. 2, p. 528, cited in Albrow, op. cit., p. 22.
14   J.S. Mill, *Considerations on Representative Government*, in J.S. Mill, *Utilitarianism, Liberty, Representative Government* (Everyman's Library), London, 1960, p. 246.
15   Herbert Spencer, 'The Coming Slavery', one of four essays in the *Contemporary Review*, republished in 1885 as *Man Versus the State*; cf. the Thinker's Library repr. 2nd edn, London, 1950, p. 40. For this citation and Montague and Muir, cf. Albrow, op. cit., pp. 25–6.

Individual Liberty (1884), developed the same theme, distinguishing the regulated servitude in which the citizens of continental bureaucracies lived from the identification between administration and the community assured in England by Parliament, the law courts and municipal liberties. For Ramsay Muir, writing on 'Bureaucracy in England' in 1910, the persistent and powerful influence of great permanent officials in the government of England constituted a pernicious and essentially un-English bureaucratization of British government.

The French Revolution and the development of commercial society in Europe, we have argued, later appeared to many as either inaugurating or consummating the shift from the community of *Gemeinschaft* to the atomistic individualism of the *Gesellschaft*. Where the *Gemeinschaft* elevates status, common ideology and tradition, the life of the community and human relationships, the *Gesellschaft* elevates the individual, his or her satisfactions, his or her rights. As both socialism and state interference and public administration grew in response to unbridled *laissez-faire* capitalism, the exponents of free enterprise, individual liberty and self-determination saw a new danger, no longer tied to aristocratic pretensions or the open elevation of social status and dependence. That danger was the development of bureaucratic-administrative attitudes, ideologies and structures. These elevate neither human relationships nor individuals and their demands. They emphasize rather social interests, socio-technical norms to which individuals are subordinate, the requirements of a total social province, concern or activity. Here individuals are functionaries carrying on the activity or passive recipients benefiting from it, objects and not subjects.

The paradox of capitalism lay in its principled opposition to bureaucratic management being accompanied by a process of economic development and rationalization which sought state support where it was advantageous and which led both to the bureaucratization of capitalist enterprises as they grew in size and scope and to the extension of the ideology of rational planning and calculation in social life. For Weber, bureaucrats were becoming as inescapable in business as in government. For Joseph Schumpeter, the 'trustified' firm lost the entrepreneurial spirit of capitalism and became a planned and bureaucratized institution; for many a subsequent writer, the internal economic organization and problems of General Motors and the USSR have had remarkable similarities.

The actual growth of government administration and intervention in nineteenth-century Britain, however, rested less on articles of faith ('freedom of contract' or the concern with public welfare as a principled ideology) than on public outrage over specific cases and the needs of particular situations – something that Oliver MacDonagh, as we have seen, has demonstrated. The nineteenth-century 'transformation' of law and government is a term MacDonagh would use with great caution. It is for him 'complex and multiple in form, dialectical and convoluted in development and, to a degree, involved in the same issues as we are today. The Victorians themselves, though much given to self-analysis, grossly misread many of the trends of the time and failed to allow for reversals, contradiction and complexity.'[16]

Socialism and bureaucracy

The ideology of socialism, as distinct from that of populism and egalitarianism, or from simple direct appeal to (social) justice, is a modern phenomenon. It was born of the first half of the nineteenth century in industrializing Europe. It constituted a critique of that new industrial society and its base in private ownership – a critique made in the light of the ideals and hopes of the French Revolution. It called for liberty, equality and fraternity, for human self-realization and self-determination at the concrete social and economic and not only at the formal constitutional and political level. It rejected, at least initially, all forms of external domination: by rulers, by represssive laws, by police force. But it found the key to the evils of the new capitalist society in private property, especially in the means of production. It rejected 'exploitation' – living off the labour of others – and private property in modern conditions as conferring the increased power to do so. But socialism proceeded to distinguish itself from populism and anarchism by accepting and indeed proclaiming

16   Oliver MacDonagh, '"Pre-transformations": Victorian Britain', in E. Kamenka and A.E.-S. Tay, eds, *Law and Social Control*, London, 1980, pp. 117–32 at p. 131.

the liberating potential of the new science and the new technology. It believed in progress and in the overwhelming significance, in human history, of the new industrial age. The age required new moralities, new forms of social organization. It would thus make possible previously undreamt-of affluence and the elimination of the power of some men over others. The radical sects of the French Revolution and Babeuf's Conspiracy of Equals were important and influential precursors of French socialism and early communism at least, but they had as yet no real conception of an industrial society. That came in the 1820s and 1830s, when socialism proper was born, primarily in England and in France. It took to itself the labour theory of value developed in England by David Ricardo and the socialist Ricardians, the concept of exploitation and a savage critique of the social dislocation introduced by unchecked greed and private interests in the new industrial cities and barracks. This was a critique foreshadowed by Rousseau, who saw the modern city as a desert populated by wild animals.

Much of this new socialist ideology (though certainly not all of it) was derived from or inspired by the thought of Saint-Simon (1760–1825), whose disciples edited the Saint-Simonian newspaper *Le Globe*. They were, like Robert Owen's followers in England and a few Italians, the first to use the words 'socialism' and 'socialist' to characterize those who recognized, correctly in *Le Globe's* view, that property must be converted into a social and not a private function. Society, the Saint-Simonians thought, needs to be planned and administered as a giant workshop. Central to Saint-Simon's often perceptive and prescient but remarkably disorganized thought was the belief that society of his day presented an 'extraordinary phenomenon: a nation which is essentially industrial, yet whose government is essentially feudal'.[17] Feudal society, feudal institutions and feudal *mores* required and were therefore dominated by men of the sword organizing the society for war. They ruled by authoritarian command backed by force. Industrial society, in contrast, is concerned with production and the harmony, cooperation and peace that are necessary for production. It has produced a new

17 *Oeuvres complètes de Saint-Simon et Enfantin*, Aalen, 1963–4, vol. XXXVII, p. 33, cited in Martin Krygier, 'Saint-Simon, Marx and the Non-Governed Society', in Kamenka and Krygier, eds, op. cit., pp. 34–60 at p. 35.

class of *industriels* engaged in production, whether as workers or as owners and managers, who simply follow the requirements of industry, who work associatively, 'united by the general interests of production, by the needs that they all have for security in work and freedom of trade'.[18] In modern conditions, such men – scientists, engineers, doctors, pharmacists, seamen, clock-makers, farmers and bankers, for instance – are the most essential and useful to the nation, while the traditional great offices of the crown – marshals, cardinals, archbishops and bishops, prefects and sub-prefects, government employees, judges and rich non-working proprietors – make no significant contribution to the good of the state or of society and can easily be spared. That, at least, was the theme of his famous *Parabole*, published, by coincidence, just before the assassination of the Duc de Berry in 1820 and therefore almost landing Saint-Simon in prison as having incited the assassination.

For Saint-Simon and many of his followers, the administration of an industrial society would be a rational activity and would be seen as such by those affected. It would not be based on coercion or domination, but on the acceptance of common technological means and production goals by both the industrialist and his workers. Saint-Simon himself coined the phrase, repeated by Engels and many others, that in a fully developed rationally organized industrial society the government of men will give way to the administration of things. By 1842 the communist Wilhelm Weitling, soon to call for instant revolution, was writing in his *Guarantees of Harmony and Freedom*, 'a perfect society has not a government but an administration'. Saint-Simon himself, full of plans for canals, had placed bankers as entrepreneurs and financial administrators at the apex of his social pyramid, but his actual banker friends in Restoration Paris soon became alarmed at his subversive views on property and other matters. His concept of rational administration did appeal to some of the graduates of the new Ecole Polytechnique and spread to rationally-minded reformers in Germany.

Saint-Simon, especially in his earlier works, thought that government in an industrial society would have only minimal policing functions. It would protect workers from the unproductive

18 Saint-Simon, *Oeuvres complètes*, vol. XIX, p. 47, as cited in Krygier, 'Saint-Simon', p. 39.

activities of idlers and speculators, and it would maintain order, security and freedom in production – matters that could in time become the collective responsibility of all citizens. All else is not government but management. The 'immortal' Adam Smith, Saint-Simon thought, had shown that industry developed spontaneously by internal forces and that external meddling only retarded and distorted this development. Proper administration was the recognition of the objective requirements of industry and production. The Saint-Simonian Bazard, in the lectures later assembled in the *Exposition* of Saint-Simonian doctrine, called for public ownership of the means of production and recognized that this involved the creation of a substantial and pervasive directing authority for society:

> If, as we proclaim, mankind is moving toward a state in which all individuals will be classed according to their capacities and remunerated according to their work, it is evident that the right of property, as it exists, must be abolished, because, by giving to a certain class of men the chance to live on the labor of others and in complete idleness, it preserves the exploitation of one part of the population, the most useful one, that which works and produces, in favor of those who only destroy ...
>
> [Then] A *social* institution is charged with these functions which today are so badly performed; it is the *depository* of all the instruments of production; it presides over the exploitation of all the material resources; from its vantage point it has a comprehensive view of the whole which enables it to perceive at one and the same time all parts of the industrial workshop ...
>
> The social institution of the future will direct all industries in the interest of the whole society, and especially of the peaceful laborers. We call this institution provisionally the general banking system, while entering all reservations against the too narrow interpretation which one might give to this term.
>
> The system will include in the first instance a central bank which constitutes the government in the material sphere; this bank will become the depository of all wealth, of the entire productive fund, of all instruments of production, in short of everything that today makes up the mass of private property.[19]

19 *Doctrine de Saint-Simon, Exposition* (originally published by Saint-Simon's disciples in 1830 and 1831), new edn with introduction and notes by Celestin Bouglé and Elie Halévy, Paris, 1924, pp. 255, 261, 272–3, as translated in George Lichtheim, *The Origins of Socialism*, London, 1969, pp. 52–3. Saint-Simon's own use of the term *industriels* combined into a single social class or interest group the industrial entrepreneur,

These views were incorporated in, but in Marx's view also superseded by, the thought of Karl Marx and in his vision of the ultimate society of communism – a society where the need for external coercion and the bases for political conflict would disappear. There all decisions would be collective. In an 'association of free producers' they could be reached without acrimony because they would follow from the need of human beings as such and from the activities they engaged in. The subsequently disgraced Soviet jurist E.B. Pashukanis put it most clearly in his *General Theory of Law and Marxism* (1924) when he distinguished law as the necessarily contradictory attempt to reconcile and regulate the demands of separate and conflicting juridical subjects, representing the abstract individualism of buyers and sellers competing in and for a market, from scientific administration as the application of socio-technical norms. Society under communism would be administered like a hospital, where the administrator is guided by the rules of health and the function and purpose of a hospital.

Socialists in the nineteenth century, before they attained government, had no time for bureaucracy and bureaucrats or, rather, for what they were more likely to call the state and its officials. Saint-Simon complained that officials saw government posts as theirs by right and not as sources of duties. These officials served their own interests and not the interests of those governed. They wanted high pay for themselves and extracted high taxes from the people. Useless parasites, they 'live on the work of others, either they are given or they take; . . . they are idlers, that is to say, thieves'.[20]

Karl Marx, in his early manuscript critique of Hegel's *Philosophy of Right* (1843), when he was still a philosophical radical rather than an economic determinist, accused Hegel of treating the state and its officials (*Regierungsgewalt und Staatsbeamten*) purely formalistically, as a bureaucracy. (Marx used the term

---

the scientist and manager and the industrial worker. His disciples in the 1820s were calling for the conversion of private property from an absolute right into a social function. Their incipient socialist critique of bourgeois society flowered into socialism in the 1830s. The *Exposition* and Bazard's public lectures familiarized the French public with the central tenets of the new faith – public ownership and the abolition of social inequality; *Le Globe*, the journal of the Saint-Simonian, Leroux, coined the term *socialisme* in February 1832.

20 Saint-Simon, *Oeuvres complètes*, vol. XVIII, p. 130, as cited in Krygier, 'Saint-Simon', p. 37.

Bürokratie; Hegel did not.) Hegel, Marx claimed, separated the state and bureaucracy from civil society without giving the concept of bureaucracy any concrete content apart from that of formality and formalism. He failed to show that the state or its bureaucracy were in any sense the consummation or perfection of civil society. On the contrary, the actual bureaucratic mentality and its central organizing principle of hierarchy made the bureaucracy a powerful source of abuse, encouraging internal dependence, secrecy and the creation of barriers against outsiders. Bureaucracy was not, as Hegel claimed, the *universal* estate or corporation concretizing and embodying reason and concern for the common good. It was a *particular* closed society within the state; it served its own and *not* the general interest. It treated society as material to be shaped; it imposed its own will or that of the state upon it. It represented at best an illusory general interest, for the existence and the power of bureaucracy were made possible only by the insoluble contradictions of civil society, by the irreconcilability of particular interests. It did not replace these by a general interest; it simply added another particular interest. When it was seized with enthusiasm for a 'general' interest, it could impose that only by force, by terror, from outside (Marx's criticism of Robespierre). Both state and bureaucracy were a product of alienation, of the separation of community interest from the community itself. As a result, that interest falls into other, sectional hands, becomes a private interest.

As Marx turned more concretely to politics, in the *Eighteenth Brumaire of Louis Bonaparte* (1852), for example, he continued to stress that the state's executive power, with its enormous bureaucratic and military organization – 'this appalling parasitic body which enmeshes the body of French society like a net and chokes all its pores' – separates every common interest from society as such, makes it an object of government activity. Bureaucracies, for Marx, can become powerful and almost autonomous – but only politically, never economically – when there is a stalemate in the class war and the bourgeoisie needs the state for survival. According to Marx, this happened in France in 1850 because the bourgeoisie had already lost and the working class had not yet acquired the capacity to rule the nation. Marx's recognition, at various periods of his life, that the Chinese state evolved on the basis of managerial power and not ownership has been treated by most of his disciples as fatally undermining his definition of class and his main view of history as class struggle. Shlomo Avineri, however, in *The Social and Political Thought of Karl Marx* (Cambridge, 1968) argued that Marx was far from overlooking the fact that bureaucracy and the state were becoming central phenomena of modern social and political life. (Marx had planned a special volume on the state for his initial project of a six-volume work on political economy, of which *Das Kapital* is only part.) In his letter to Kugelmann of 12 April 1871, Marx made the degree of bureaucratization of a society determine the degree of violence the proletariat would need to overthrow its ruling class. In England, the United States and perhaps the Netherlands, he wrote, there were better chances for a peaceful transition to proletarian control; in the bureaucratic societies in other parts of the continent there would have to be violent revolution aimed at the bureaucratic structure itself. Certainly, in the same year Marx was saying, in his *Civil War in France* and especially in the drafts of that essay on the Paris Commune, that earlier revolutions had only perfected the state machinery instead of throwing off that dreaded incubus. The working class, he now believed, could not simply lay hold of the ready-made state machinery and wield it for its own purpose – it would have to smash it. Marx did not at any stage think that administrative functions would simply wither away. They would be needed in the new society, but as Martin Krygier has reminded us, and as Chinese Maoists stressed during their 'Great Proletarian Cultural Revolution', they would be simple administrative functions, divided between central and communal institutions and subject to popular control through the communes. Functionaries would also survive, at least in the transition to socialism; but they would be paid less, their tenure would be less secure and the general cost of administration not directly appertaining to production would be significantly diminished from the outset. In factories themselves, the present barracks-like discipline, with its overseers, its supervising officers and sergeants, would be replaced by cooperation and coordination. There would be authority but it would be the rational voluntarily accepted authority required in all forms of cooperation. It would not be imposed by capitalists standing outside the process of production and not participating in it. The commanding will, as Krygier puts it,[21] would resemble that of an orchestra conductor and not that of a field commander. This would be even more so since the unwilling and alienated detail worker, prevented from seeing the process of production as a whole, would be superseded by an individual with all-round development. An association of producers would take the place of coercive direction by political and economic bosses. Administration, Marx seemed to think, would be confined to production – though his famous formula 'to each according to his contribution' in socialism, and 'to each according to his needs' in communism implied more than that unless distribution is incorporated within production.

Socialism from the beginning held together disparate and conflicting hopes and beliefs. The conflict between them was evinced from time to time in bitter struggles between the elevation of the general social interest and that of the working class, between centralization and spontaneity, evolutionary socialism and revolutionary communism, between Marxists and anarchists, between state socialism and syndicalism. Behind all this lay the fundamental tension between the socialist elevation of the informal community, of the status-less, unauthoritarian *Gemeinschaft*, on the one hand, and of centralized planning and control, of the bureaucratic-administrative planned society, on the other. In western Europe, by the late nineteenth century, the majority labour movement that was to form the Second International was coming to see democratic elections and the capture of state power through the ballot-box as the proper, irresistible course for socialism in the West. The state would not wither away but would be used democratically by the working masses to protect their interests and those of society as a whole, to nationalize at least the commanding heights of industry and commerce – banks, railways, heavy industry and much else. (Agriculture was a matter of dissension, where socialists were split between mechanizing and centralizing policies, including land nationalization, meant to turn farmers into industrial workers on large estates, or leasing and distributing land and liberating, economically, the poorer farmer to create a productive smallholder's agriculture on a cooperative and not a collective basis.) Generally, however, mainstream democratic socialism in

21 Krygier, 'Saint-Simon', p. 59.

the leading industrial countries of the West at the end of the nineteenth century and since has stood for the constant extension of the public sector and of public employment and for the consequent increase in state and administrative intervention in all aspects of the community's life. It reconciled the initial tension between socialism as the elevation of the public interest and socialism (especially early communism) as elevating the proletariat against other classes by treating the working masses as the vast majority of mankind. Democracy and socialist policies, the opening of careers to all talented individuals and an egalitarianism that would reject unearned authority – the authority of origin or wealth – would be sufficient, many believed, to convert the bureaucracies of the past into genuine bodies of public servants and the state into what indeed finally became, in some countries, the welfare state.

On the Left, the criticism of this elevation of the democratic state and its public service as capable of serving, relatively selflessly, the public interest came primarily from the anarchists and from the communists when speaking of states not run by them, states in which private owners had not been expropriated. The criticism began already in Marx's day with Bakunin's insistence that a workers' state would be a state administered by ex-workers and as oppressive as any other. It was given impetus by the anarcho-syndicalist and Sorelian attacks on 'parliamentary socialism' as a betrayal of socialism. It was consummated by the Polish revolutionary Jan Waclaw Machajski (1866/7–1926), whose pamphlets written in Siberian exile and published later as *The Intellectual Worker* (1904) charged that socialism was no longer the ideology of the working class but that of 'white-handed' administrators who wanted to use the conception of a social interest to extract surplus value from the masses and feather their own nests. They were able to do so because, in the new conditions of modern society, education was a form of property and they sought to keep education to themselves. This new educated class, originally servants of feudalism and then of capitalism, now wanted to become the new masters, appropriating more and more of the national product and using 'scientific' socialism as an ideological justification for elevating themselves and for extracting 'surplus value' from the worker:

in every country, in every state, there exists a huge class of people who have neither industrial nor commercial capital and yet live like real masters. They own neither land nor factories nor workshops, but they enjoy a robber's income no smaller than that of the middling and large capitalists. They do not have their own enterprises, but they are white-hands just like the middling and large capitalists. They too spend their whole lives free from manual labour and if they do participate in production then it is only as managers, directors, engineers. That is, in relation to the workers, to the slaves of manual labour, they are commanders and masters, just like the capitalist proprietors.[22]

In spite of Machajski – whose views have had more impact on socialist critics of the Soviet Union and on those who used the concept of managerial society in the 1930s and 1940s than on the western labour movement – the support in socialist circles for the extension of state services and state control did not diminish in western societies, at least until very recently. In fact, public servants in modern industrial and post-industrial societies in the West have grown so much in number and include so high a proportion of comparatively low level employees (including clerks and tradesmen) that they do not see themselves and are not seen by others as a caste lording it over society, running the state and inheriting and exercising for themselves its authority and claim to respect. Many western radicals, indeed, now see the increasing numbers of public servants, teachers, welfare workers, etc., as a source of 'contradiction in the capitalist state' – as promoting, in defiance of their formal meliorating role in the 'capitalist system', the ideology of social care and cooperation, and bringing the 'capitalist' welfare state to a crisis.

On the other hand, the ordinary citizen does find him or herself increasingly confronted by a veritable host of complex and detailed regulations interpreted and enforced by quite modestly placed civil servants. The result is an increasing hostility to bureaucratization rather than to bureaucrats, a rejection of the application of general rules to individual cases. In many democracies, and more recently elsewhere, this has led to a

22 Jan Waclaw Machajski, *Burzhuaznaia revoliutsiia i rabochee delo*, St Petersburg, 1906, p. 86, as translated in Marshall Shatz, 'Jan Waclaw Machajski: The "Conspiracy" of the Intellectuals', *Survey*, No. 62, 1967, pp. 45–57 at pp. 48–9.

modification (at least partly, but not wholly, cosmetic) of the bureaucratic working style to emphasize decentralization, informality and accessible explanation – that is, to a much less directive style and an emphasis on social service as counselling. The delegation of discretion to ignore or modify the rules is obviously a very difficult problem in the provision of mass services and is in fact still severely limited. The tendency, rather, has been to elevate and to make more accessible information and complaints officers, to emphasize public relations and to regularize and extend appeal procedures even in quite minor matters. The provision of independent review through ombudsmen and the growth of administrative appeals tribunals in many fields is a further development. Similar trends, though still much more limited, are beginning to manifest themselves in the far more rigidly bureaucratized communist countries and to gain the suport of reform-minded leaders. Against this, as we shall see in chapter 5, stands a new trend, away from legally trained, rule-bound bureaucrats, to the elevation of bureaucracy as 'rational', economic, resource-allocation, as 'money management', in an atmosphere of increasingly strident demand both for money and for the economical use of state resources.

Bureaucracy in the USSR

The history of revolutionary socialism – i.e., of modern communism – has been a different matter. Communist revolutions, beginning with Lenin's seizure of power in Petrograd in October 1917, have not taken place in advanced industrialized societies or in democratic settings, except where they have been imposed from above – as in Czechoslovakia – by foreign victors. (Yugoslavia is to some extent an exception.) The Russian Revolution, like the French Revolution of 1789–99, inspired Franz Borkenau's law of the two-fold development of revolutions: 'They begin as anarchistic movements against the existing bureaucratic State organization, which they inevitably destroy; they continue by setting in its place another, in most cases stronger bureaucratic organization, which suppresses all free mass movements.'[23] Indeed, as Benedict Anderson was to stress some forty-five years later:

> for over 65 years CPSU leaders have made policy in the Kremlin, ancient citadel of Czarist power – out of all possible sites in the socialist state's vast territories. Similarly, the PRC's capital is that of the Manchus (while Chiang Kai-shek had moved it to Nanking) and the CCP leaders congregate in the Forbidden City of the Sons of Heaven. . . . Like the complex electrical-system in any large mansion when the owner has fled, the state awaits the new owner's hand at the switch to be very much its old brilliant self again.[24]

It is now a commonplace that communist revolutions have taken place and been comparatively successful not in advanced industrial societies but in backward agrarian ones, suffering the dislocation of initial commercialization and industrialization, usually revealed by the previous government's incapacity in war. Leninist communism, in short, has been an alternative route to modernization and industrialization. It is, for a period, most useful and initially more acceptable in those countries where the state has traditionally been the innovator and director in the economy and in the society as a whole and where other social classes have been too weakly developed to confront it or to act independently of it. Hence, communist revolutions, for all the anarchism of Lenin's *State and Revolution* and of the ideology of the period of War Communism (1918–21), have been disciplined and calculating seizures of power, meant to transform society through state action from above. The result has been the almost total bureaucratization of the new society – more pervasive and more efficient than the backward-looking bureaucracies of the past – especially in the Soviet Union. Bureaucratization had been demanded in the name of and made necessary by the twin goals of pervasive political control and rapid economic mobilization.

Behind the growth of bureaucracy and the renewed elevation of the state in the Soviet Union, however, lay the political

23 Franz Borkenau, 'State and Revolution in the Paris Commune, the Russian Revolution and the Spanish Civil War', *Sociological Review*, vol. XXIX, 1937, pp. 41–75 at p. 67.

24 Benedict Anderson, *Imagined Communities: Reflections on the Origin and Spread of Nationalism*, London, 1983, p. 145.

elevation of the Communist Party and the doctrine of the dictatorship of the proletariat, necessitating the destruction of all 'class enemies'. Already in December 1917, Lenin, ruling with a Council of People's Commissars, set up the Extraordinary Commission, the Cheka, later renamed the OGPU, i.e. NKVD, the MVD and the KGB. It was set up not by statute but on the basis of hasty and incomplete notes of a meeting of the council. Its functions were to stop and liquidate all attempts at and acts of counter-revolution and sabotage. It was to bring saboteurs and counter-revolutionaries before revolutionary tribunals and to work out measures for the struggle against them. Within a few months, all other socialist parties were included within the definition of counter-revolutionaries and saboteurs. The foundation of a pervasive network of espionage and repression had thus been laid. A 1918 Decree, indeed, inaugurated the Red Terror under that name – it gave the Cheka power to isolate enemies in concentration camps and established special chambers of the Cheka to deal with 'parasitic elements constituting a social danger but not guilty of specific criminal acts'. The work of the central Cheka was later supplemented, despite changes of name, by provincial and republican Chekas, but with strict control from the centre. It was at the very beginning of the Soviet regime, too, that the system of special rations and privileged access to apartments, goods, clubs and leisure resorts for loyal party workers was devised – supplementary in a crucial respect to the comparatively egalitarian salary system and necessary, it was said, to save busy and responsible comrades, labouring for the common good, time in queuing. Like the Cheka, it was only to blossom.

In 1921, the Soviet government, appalled by the breakdown of the economy during the period of War Communism including the Civil War, proclaimed the New Economic Policy, encouraging state-licensed economic development on a capitalist basis. On the political front, however, ruthless centralization and administrative controls continued – in education, in literature and the press, in trade unions and public organizations and in the party itself. In 1919 already, the Eighth Congress of the Communist Party introduced five of the nine departments envisaged as forming its new administrative machinery. Three of those were both important and indicative of the party's organizational sophistication in building, consciously and deliberately, an apparatus. Those were the Department of Information and Statistics (*Informotdel*), which was to obtain full information from local party committees on their structure, methods and activities; Organization and Instruction (*Orgotdel*), responsible for devising and establishing institutional forms for supervising the working of the party apparatus; and Records and Assignments (*Uchraspred*), to collect information about party members as a basis for central appointments and staff allocations. *Informotdel* a year later was absorbed into *Orgotdel* and the remaining two departments were amalgamated in 1923 to form an effective and powerful network used by Stalin, with great skill, to secure domination over the party and the state. In 1927, with the abolition of the NEP, both the ideology and the reality of total bureaucratization of the society at large took a giant leap through the Five Year Plans. The brutal reality of the forced collectivization of the peasants in 1929 destroyed the last vestiges of economic or ideological independence by any major social group in the Soviet Union. The first and the last free election had been held in 1918 and its results – victory for the Social Revolutionary (peasant) party – ignored. Within a few more years, Stalin had not only totally bureaucratized the party and the society, including the organization and supervision of the unions, but eliminated all rivals, oppositionist and critical factions or individuals. That done, he proclaimed, in 1936, that socialism had been achieved.

The new theory was that the state and the dictatorship of the proletariat still could not wither away until the working class victory had become worldwide. The function of military suppression inside the country, Stalin wrote in 1940, had ceased by 1936. The state had only to protect social property from thieves and pilferers. But it still had to defend the country from foreign attack and penetration and therefore required the Red Army and Navy, the punitive organs and intelligence services (dealing with spies, assassins and wreckers allegedly sent in from abroad). The functions of economic organization and cultural education by the state organs remained, and were now elevated still further. The socialist state was now proclaimed to be a mighty force aiding the material transformation of the economic base. It did so, and basically allegedly still does so, by organizing, administering and controlling, directly through ministries, indirectly through the party and party-controlled watchdog organizations, all significant aspects of economic, political, social and cultural life in the Soviet Union. If bureaucracy means, as Laski put it, 'a system of government, the control of which is so completely in the hands of officials that their power jeopardizes the liberty of ordinary citizens', then the Soviet Union has been the most pervasive and efficient bureaucracy in world history since the Inca empire – efficient, though, in terms only of political goals and in the achievement of specific limited economic projects at whatever cost may be necessary. Even then it is that no longer.

For historians and sociologists, the existence of a highly bureaucratized state and the reappearance of one in the Soviet Union is not a source of puzzlement or difficulty. For Marxists, who insist on subordinating the political to the economic in their theoretical writing (if not in their practice) and who regard bureaucracies as nothing more than transmission belts between the rulers (an economic class) and the ruled, it is. How did the toiling masses – peasants and workers – come to be the ruled, and not the rulers, in a workers' state, subordinated to an all-powerful and greatly privileged bureaucracy? And what class, if any, did this bureaucracy – which itself owned none of the means of production – constitute or represent?

Official Soviet ideology, of course, has insisted that there is no bureaucratic class or caste in the Soviet Union but only a stratum of the intelligentsia which works with a pen or with its mind rather than with its hands. That stratum, the theory runs, serves the working people and the socialist interest in the same way as everyone else. Lenin wrote but did not complete his *State and Revolution* in the second half of 1916 and in August/September 1917, a month before the Bolshevik coup made him head of government. In this pamphlet he encouraged the view that a Bolshevik revolution would mean the coming of a stateless, unbureaucratic society in which every cook could be a politician. Social administration and accounting would be carried out by everyone who knew that 2 + 2 makes 4. There would be an instant enormous expansion of real democracy. The state would not wither away immediately, but the 'masses' would be drawn into its work. It would be a proletarian state – a dictatorship of the proletariat indeed – replacing the dictatorial bourgeois state.

It would be needed as long as there was threat of counter-revolution, as long as bourgeois habits had not entirely disappeared and as long as the principle of 'From each according to his capacity, to each according to his contribution' had not yet been replaced by the ultimate communist principle 'From each according to his capacity, to each according to his needs'. Until then, the narrow horizon of bourgeois right and the necessity to calculate 'with the cold heartedness of a Shylock' would not have been transcended.

Lenin did insist, even in this, his most 'anarchist' work, that the dictatorship of the proletarian state would have important supervisory and administrative functions. These would be the suppression of the minority of exploiters and counter-revolutionaries; the control of production and distribution; and keeping accounts of labour time and the products produced. Suppression would be carried out with a very simple, minimal 'machine', almost without any special apparatus. It would be done by the 'organization of the armed masses' – such, says Lenin, as the Soviet of Workers and Soldiers Deputies. (In fact, as we have seen, the Cheka was established within a few months and its successor organizations have reached totals of probably a million organized and hierarchically controlled functionaries and troops.) Control of production and keeping account of labour and products, Lenin thought, could be done immediately by the armed population. All citizens would become employees and workers of a single nationwide 'syndicate'. The accounting and control necessary had already been simplified by capitalism to the extreme; now it would be reduced to 'the extraordinarily simple operations – which any literate persons can perform – of supervising and recording, knowledge of the four rules of arithmetic and issuing of appropriate receipts'. (*Gosplan*, dozens of All-Union and Republican ministries, People's Control, Party Control, supervision by central bodies, republican bodies and local soviets have expanded at a rate even greater than that with which police functions expanded, to the extent, indeed, that the Soviet Union is universally thought of as one of the most bureaucratized societies in the modern world.)

Lenin did insist, in *State and Revolution*, and in practice from 1918 onward, that factory discipline would be required in the first phase of communism. It would be extended to the whole of society, but only as a necessary step for thoroughly purging society of the 'infamies' and 'abominations' of capitalist exploitation. Neither could management within industry simply disappear. Managerial positions, however, would become accessible to all; the authority of managers would be limited by workers' control, egalitarian pay scales and election and recall. It was clear to Lenin, however, that technological production in modern society required a scientifically trained staff of engineers, agronomists etc. Their work would be essentially unchanged: 'these gentlemen are working today in obedience to the wishes of capitalists and will work even better tomorrow in obedience to the wishes of the armed workers.'[25]

By March 1918, however, as Krygier and many others stress, Lenin was emphasizing that administration generally had become the main and central task of the state. It required 'a single state Bank, the biggest of the big'[26] and 'the transformation of the whole state economic mechanism into a single huge machine'.[27] Contemptuous as he had always been of Russian sloth and inefficiency – *bezlabornost* – he emphasized the need for efficiency, for a knowledge of organization on a scale of millions, for the need to learn the techniques of management, industrial production and trade possessed by managers of trusts, the big organizers of capitalism.[28] Many aspects of Lenin's vision for the new society were profoundly practical and startlingly Saint-Simonian. He insisted that the former writers of underground pamphlets and orators of the revolution militant were not well trained to be administrators of the revolution triumphant. Initially the revolution, in building the new society, would have to employ those who were qualified, no matter what their past politics. Such specialists of all kinds would need to be paid higher salaries during the transitional period, for it was obvious that an unskilled labourer or a cook could not immediately get on with the job of state administration.[29]

T.H. Rigby has reminded us that despite 'Lenin's constant stress on the *non-bureaucratic* character of the new proletarian

---

25   V.I. Lenin, *Collected Works*, Moscow, 1964, vol. XXV, p. 473.
26   Ibid., vol. XXVI, p. 106.
27   Ibid., vol. XXVII, pp. 90–1.
28   Ibid., vol. XLII, p. 77.
29   Ibid., vol. XXVI, p. 113. I have drawn, for some of the Lenin citations, on Martin Krygier, 'Weber, Lenin and the Reality of Socialism', in Kamenka and Krygier, eds, op. cit., pp. 61–87, at pp. 76, 78, 80.

state, the task of equipping itself with an effective bureaucracy was in fact the main preoccupation of the Soviet state during its initial phase, and predominantly this expressed itself in efforts to "take over" and "set in motion" the old ministerial machine.'[30] Lenin, in the face of strong opposition, persuaded the Ninth Party Congress in January 1920 that collegial discussion of questions preliminary to execution must be distinguished from the establishment of the most strict personal responsibility for executive functions. These must be directed by a single final authority in each enterprise even if one-man management was 'dictatorial'. By the end of 1920, 86 per cent of all Soviet enterprises had been placed under one-man authority in spite of the criticism of such 'dictatorship' by leading Bolkshevik figures, including Bukharin and Preobrazhensky.

Even (or especially) after the revolution, Lenin did continue to attack bureaucracy, bureaucratism and bureaucratic methods in Soviet government. He attacked abuses, excesses and inefficiencies, not the existence of bureaucratic structures and functions. The flaws he attacked and identified with bureaucratism and bureaucratic methods, as Martin Krygier has reminded us,[31] were of three kinds: (a) predilection for authoritarian dictation from above: for 'bossing' and 'ordering' (a predilection Lenin ascribed to Trotsky); (b) intellectualist and bureaucratic 'projecteering', drawing up utopian plans not subjected to any realistic tests of their practicability or assessment of their effects; (c) bureaucratism as red tape and mismanagement, as the capacity of administrators to foul up everything that is working without their intervention. When Lenin now attacked 'bureaucracy' or *chinovnichestvo* in the Soviet state, he had in mind, primarily, a *working style*.

In the 1920s, the Soviet Union's leading intellectual oppositionist and anti-Stalinist, Leon Trotsky, did warn the party against a new phenomenon threatening its work. This was the spread of 'bureaucratism' which was the result of the transfer to the party élite of the methods and administrative manners accumulated during recent years. He complained of the fundamentally

30 T.H. Rigby, 'Birth of the Central Soviet Bureaucracy', *Politics*, vol. VII, 1972, pp. 121–35 at p. 124.

31 Krygier, 'Weber, Lenin', p. 83, drawing on Daniel Tarschys, *Beyond the State: The Future Polity in Classical and Soviet Marxism*, Stockholm, 1972, and Adam Ulam, *Lenin and the Bolsheviks*, Glasgow, 1975.

improper and unhealthy regime within the party and of its 'secretarial bureaucratism'. He attacked the growth in power of party secretaries – Stalin was the chief of them – who controlled appointments to all divisions of the party and the state. He complained of the extent to which bureaucratization was detaching the leaders from the masses and creating a new 'party secretary psychology', so that 'leadership takes on a purely organizational character and frequently degenerates into order-giving and meddling'. For Trotsky at this stage – 1923 – this new bureaucratism was essentially a matter of manners, of bad manners, acquired in administration and not in political, agitational work with the 'masses'. Both Lenin and his wife, Krupskaya, had made that charge against Stalin, but treated it as a personality defect. Trotsky, aware of its wider implications, suggested that 'the source of bureaucratism resides in the growing concentration of the party's attention and efforts upon the governmental institutions and apparatuses and in the slowness of the development of industry.'[32] For, as Trotsky had argued in the articles collected as *Literature and Revolution*, 'backwardness by itself bred bad manners'.[33] (The Russian term *nekul'turnost'* is now used in the USSR to condemn roughness, 'uncouthness'.)

Much of Trotsky's argument at this period emphasized the psychological attitudes created by immersion in administrative tasks in the context of a hierarchical state apparatus also gaining control over the party. He contrasted these, as David Lovell says, with an idealized version of the allegedly democratic political climate and attitudes of Lenin and 'true' Bolshevism. With the retirement of Lenin from political life, the contrast had become worse, according to Trotsky; his own battle against bureaucratism and for a 'new course' was conducted within the party until his expulsion. After that, in exile and until he was murdered at Stalin's command, he vacillated between various versions of the view that the degeneration of the Bolshevik Party under Stalin, and the 'betrayal' of the revolution, were more than a matter of mere psychology, but did not constitute the birth of a new social formation. The retirement of Lenin from political leadership,

32 In Leon Trotsky, *The Challenge of the Left Opposition (1923–25)*, ed. Naomi Allen, New York, 1975, pp. 52, 55, 75, 77. For a discussion of these citations and others, see David Lovell, *Trotsky's Analysis of Soviet Bureaucratization: A Critical Essay*, London, 1985, passim, esp. pp. 9–29.

33 Lovell, op. cit., p. 18.

Trotsky now thought, had been followed by a Thermidorean reaction – which meant not just a downswing in revolutionary enthusiasm, but a re-emergence of suspect groups and attitudes. As Stalin's power grew, 'Bonapartism' became another term that Trotsky used, sometimes distinguishing it from Thermidorean-ism and sometimes conflating the two. Trotsky emphasized the failure of the revolution in Russia to spread to the industrially advanced countries of Europe, the resultant isolation of the Soviet Union in a capitalist world and the massive contradictions to be overcome in the attempt to establish socialism in a backward country as an explanation for this trend. That was to become commonplace in thinking Marxist circles, and is by now accepted even by the USSR as the normal explanation for admitted shortcomings. Trotsky recognized half-heartedly that these explanations postulated institutional and not only psycho-logical bases for bureaucracy. The fault of the post-Lenin leadership, of Stalin in particular, he thought, was to encourage the formation of a distinct and privileged group of professional bureaucrats, to surrender to its passion for power and privilege. Stalin failed to take steps to ensure that the bureaucracy was no more than a scaffolding, to be pulled down when it was no longer needed.

The Marxist framework within which he worked prevented Trotsky from ever seeing the bureaucracy as a class. At most it derived support from what he saw as other Bonapartist castes – *kulaks*, he thought at one stage, diplomats, the army and navy, etc. The bureaucracy, for Trotsky, was an administrative staff 'indissolubly bound up with a ruling economic class, feeding itself upon the social roots of the latter, maintaining itself and falling together with it'.[34] Primarily, as Lovell argues, Trotsky 'explained the role of the Stalinist bureaucracy, and the con-sequences of its rule, in political, not sociological, terms. It had an administrative and not a productive function.'[35] For Trotsky in his later life, bureaucrats ruled only politically, not economic-ally. Until his death, Trotsky continued to regard the Soviet Union as economically a socialist society, a workers' state, in which a

34 *Writings of Leon Trotsky (1933–4)*, New York, 1972, pp. 112–13; cf. Martin Krygier, 'The Revolution Betrayed? From Trotsky to the New Class', in Kamenka and Krygier, eds, op. cit., p. 97.
35 Lovell, op. cit., p. 45, drawing on Trotsky's *The Revolution Betrayed*.

bureaucratic caste, an overwhelming, incompetent and expensive caste, robbed the workers and destroyed the morality of the Communist Party. That caste remained, for Trotsky, a social parasite. It was compelled to defend state property and the socialist economic system as the sources of its power and income. It could not be an independent economic class, the basis of a new social formation. Trotsky's theory of that caste, and of Thermidorianism and Bonapartism, was neither systematically developed nor given consistent and coherent exposition; he knew only that a political phenomenon bureaucracy could not have an independent history or an independent future. To think that would be un-Marxist.

The New Class

Only in the late 1930s did some thinkers, mostly ex-Marxists, begin to see bureaucracies in modern societies, or in modern societies of a certain sort, as new ruling classes. They, too, did so hesitantly and without much theoretical depth or care. Bruno Rizzi in *La Bureaucratisation du monde* (1939) argued that the bourgeoisie was an exhausted social force. A new form of society – bureaucratic collectivism – was successfully taking over by assaulting and appropriating capitalist power and property. This had happened in the Soviet Union and – though only partly – in Nazi Germany, Fascist Italy and militarist Japan. It was also developing, Rizzi believed, in the United States through the New Deal. Under bureaucratic collectivism, the ruling bureaucracy formed a class which collectively exploited the mass of the population and drew surplus value from its work. Rizzi himself believed that bureaucratic collectivism was historically progressive, a transitional social formation between capitalism and socialism. In Lucien Laurat's *Marxism and Democracy* (London, 1940, a translation from the French original, Paris, London, 1939) and James Burnham's *The Managerial Revolution* (London, 1941), matters were taken further. Laurat pointed to the growing power of a new class – pluto-technocratic in the west and bureau-technocratic in the USSR; Burnham noted that the modern corporation was increasingly run by managers and not by its owners (who were often fragmented: trust companies, pension funds, small and large individual shareholders etc.). He saw such managers as introducing managerial societies throughout the world.

For all these writers, working out of the Marxist heritage, it was important to show that the new ruling bureaucracies were in fact owners of the means of production, through their individual or collective control, even if they were not legal owners. All of them rejected sharply Trotsky's traditional Marxist view that bureaucracies were only hirelings of a ruling class. Rizzi puts it succinctly:

> The 'clerk' who, following Trotsky, is only the transmission mechanism of imperialism, has ruled in Russia for over twenty years and rules a country which takes up a sixth of the continents, with a population of 180 millions. Obviously, the clerk has alarming proportions, much greater than those of his masters themselves. Such domination requires a 'staff' which, on the national scale, represents for us a class. To reinforce it, this class pushes its domination into all domains of society, and where it encounters resistance, bypasses it by climbing over mountains of corpses. The bureaucratic regime of the USSR has, first, sacrificed the Communist Party and the Third International, then the Red Army itself. Tasks of this magnitude cannot be done by 'cliques' or 'staffs' or 'clerks' but only by classes.[36]

The best known of the new class theorists writing after the Second World War, Milovan Djilas, also began his apostasy by insisting in newspaper articles in the early 1950s that Stalinist bureaucrats lived at the expense of direct producers who had no rights. Like traditional ruling classes, they controlled production and took a disproportionate share of the surplus for themselves. Still, this bureaucracy was not a class; it did not own the means of production in the traditional sense. It was a caste that appeared in the transition from capitalism to communism, a reactionary anti-socialist tendency that could be overthrown. It was in *The New Class*, published in 1957 – by which time Djilas had been expelled from the Yugoslav Communist Party – that he insisted that the Communist political bureaucracy was a 'collectively' owning class that had the use, enjoyment and disposition of material goods, of nationalized property, in precisely the way that

36 Bruno Rizzi, *L'URSS: collectivisme bureaucratique* [The first part of his *La Bureaucratisation du monde*], Paris, 1976, p. 48, as translated in Krygier, op. cit., p. 104.

constituted the Roman Law definition of ownership. Earlier, just before his expulsion from the Yugoslav League of Communists in 1954, he had written of the 'inner circle' of its rulers, living in a 'closed world' of automobiles and Pullman cars, restricted holiday resorts and special stores for food and clothing. That circle maintained its solidarity, 'not so much from ideological and moral unity but rather from the same way of living and similar interests, from the nature of power and the manner in which it was attained'.[37]

The discussion has not ended. Its upshot is to show that the classical Marxist definitions of classes and of the state, and the emphasis on ownership, are not adequate for the discussion of social structure and social domination, or of bureaucracy and bureaucratic regimes. Djilas and many others in the West, in Eastern Europe, the USSR and China have come to realize that. So have some Communist rulers.

37   Milovan Djilas, 'Jugoslavija', in *Borba*, 18 October 1953, p. 3, as translated in Michael Mile Lustig, *Leon Trotsky and Milovan Djilas: Critics of Soviet and Yugoslav Bureaucracy*, PhD thesis, Brown University, 1982, reproduced in facsimile by UMI, Ann Arbor, 1984, p. 214.

5

What is Bureaucracy and What is its Future?

'Bureaucracy' is an overworked concept and often an unclear one. It is, as Martin Albrow has put it, 'a term of strong emotive overtones and elusive connotations'.[1] Albrow distinguishes seven separate though related modern meanings of the term.[2] These I have in part incorporated and in part significantly amended in what follows. Most neutrally, and in my view most fundamentally, as a descriptive core, 'bureaucracy' means a centrally directed, systematically organized and hierarchically structured staff devoted to the regular, routine and efficient carrying out of large-scale administrative tasks according to policies dictated by rulers or directors standing outside and above the bureaucracy. Such a staff, as Weber rightly saw, tends to become rule-bound, functionally specialized, elevating impersonality and *esprit de corps*. But 'bureaucracy' has also meant the opposite of organizational efficiency and effective centralized control: red tape, slowness of procedure, reluctance to take a decision, the unnecessary multiplication of people, rules and forms – a connotation achieved by singling out for attention unfavourable secondary features or tendencies of bureaucratic structures. The term 'bureaucracy' has been included in, but also contrasted with, the more general concept of administration. Sometimes this is done by seeing bureaucracy as a formal and impersonal mode of administration, sometimes by seeing bureaucracy as that form of administration where administrators (the bureaucrats, the officials) have become the real rulers, arrogating to themselves privilege, power and control, and thus prejudicing, as Laski put it, the liberties of ordinary citizens or the power of their nominal ruler(s). Not only administrative forms or staffs, but whole societies have been described as 'bureaucratic' on that basis. Some writers distinguish

1 Martin Albrow, *Bureaucracy*, London, 1970, p. 13.
2 Ibid., pp. 84–105.

modern state-centred and highly or pervasively administered societies from looser, more traditional and less rationalistic societies of the past. Others single out, in both past and present, societies basically or effectively ruled by a caste of officials, who derive their position and their power from carrying out socially central administrative tasks. These have been called oriental despotisms, examples of the Asiatic mode of production, bureaucratic feudalism, state capitalism or simply 'totalitarian'. They have been contrasted with freer, less state-directed, more pluralist societies that have not been totally bureaucratized and with arbitrary personal rule, tyranny or 'sultanism', where nothing is rule-bound, routine, predictable.

Like so many fundamental concepts in social thought, each of these 'definitions' or uses of the word 'bureaucracy' incorporates a wider theory. In the case of 'rule' or 'power' of officials it further incorporates a relative, shifting standard of what amounts to 'power', best expressed as a point along a continuum stretching from helplessness to omnipotence but rarely, if ever, achieving either end. All of the uses I have mentioned, nevertheless, derive from the elevation or criticism of a basic concept of bureaucracy as referring to centrally directed and supervised, hierarchically structured routine administration on a scale so large that it must be conducted on the basis of rules, files and delegated but formally limited authority that is related to the functions of each office. Let us begin, therefore, by distinguishing sharply and definitely between the descriptive core of the term 'bureaucracy' and pejorative overtones that can be and have been added to it by incorporating further claims about the nature or effects of bureaucratic structures and organizations. Those claims may be true even if they are often grossly exaggerated, but they constitute a separate and different issue.

Max Weber was right in rejecting the usefulness and centrality for the study of history and society of rigidly defined, clear and distinct universal concepts, static pictures, against which concrete historical processes and events were to be matched and classified. He perceived, rightly, that 'bureaucracy', like many other social concepts, constituted a shorthand for complex systems and trends that work themselves out over time. They had to be understood in and through wider social contexts, functions and problems. They held together, in logical and practical relationships, mutually supporting characteristics, principles, attitudes and traditions; they struggled against that which was for them disruptive, competitive, dysfunctional. Bureaucracy, in short, was an 'ideal type', a selectively accentuated theoretical construct recognizing and organizing the existence and inter-relation of logical and historical trends – both injecting theory into practice and drawing theoretical perceptions out of it. Ideal types enable us to recognize the great conflicts of history for what they are – not mere random or accidental collisions, but great struggles between competing trends, outlooks, traditions and ways of organization, incorporating 'contradictory' principles, values and *desiderata*. For, as Werner Sombart has rightly said, 'No theory, no history'. But ideal types, though suited to studying social trends and institutions over time, are not them-selves atemporal. What is coherent, mutually supportive, 'efficient' in one age or set of circumstances may cease to be so in another, may itself give rise to unsuspected conflicts and tensions as it confronts new situations and demands.

The impact of Max Weber in giving us new perspectives on the past has been immense. He has revolutionized much writing of history and much of our understanding of past, especially of ancient, societies, just as he has profoundly influenced our appreciation of the differences that European developments in the past three centuries have made and are still making in the rest of the world. As Theodore von Laue has put it:

> [T]he world revolution of Westernization brought together, in in-escapably intimate and virtually instant interaction, all the peoples of the world, regardless of their prior cultural evolution or their capacity – or incapacity – for peaceful coexistence ...
>
> In creating an interdependent world through conquest, coloniza-tion and expanded opportunities for all ... [a small minority commonly called 'The West'] imposed its own accomplishments as a universal standard to which all others, however reluctantly, had to submit ...
>
> Western ascendancy was so complete that it left only one rational response: abject imitation as a condition of survival and self-affirmation. Decolonization and the formation of Western-inspired nation-states among the former colonial and semi-colonial peoples merely escalated the imitation and hardened the grip of Western institutions and values over the entire world. Even the most heated

protests against Western power – and they were never lacking – were expressed in Western concepts and propagated by Western technology in Western languages.

For the sake of feeding, housing, transporting, educating, and employing the world's population, 'Westernization' is now pressed forward by non-Westerners themselves. Culturally neutralized, it has become 'modernization' or simply 'development', the common goal of all peoples and governments no matter how handicapped in achieving it.[3]

Much as some may dislike the ideology of 'modernization', it is gross misunderstanding to blind oneself to the fact. The apparent challenges to the West, both communism and fascism, Laue insists, in fact tried 'to convert their subjects by force into organization-minded citizens as disciplined, loyal, and cooperative as their counterparts in the Western democracies'.[4]

Rizzi's title *La Bureaucratisation du monde*, then, was an accurate enough prediction – a *leitmotif* in recent human history and in global perspectives, made even more pervasive and inevitable by the continuing rapid escalation of the world's population and of technological means and the need for centralized controls and ever-wider economies of scale. Weber's conception of rational–legal authority and of modern bureaucracy as an ideal type has in crucial respects indeed been working itself out over history, now providing the constitutional forms, the administrative structures and the legal systems or rules of the world's nation-states, of regional and international bodies and of great multinational corporations.

Weber himself was careful to insist that no actual historical institution or administrative structure corresponds completely to its ideal type. Some of the less interesting criticism of Weber consists merely of elaboration of this fact – of bringing out the importance of personal networks, of traditions, of charisma, even of corruption in actual existing bureaucracies, both past and present. That no one sensible would deny or consider a valid or important reason for rejecting Weber's postulation of a trend. A more interesting and significant criticism emphasizes the role that personal networks, traditions, charisma and even corruption play

3 Theodore von Laue, *The World Revolution of Westernization: The Twentieth Century in Global Perspective*, New York and Oxford, 1987, pp. 3–4.

4 Ibid., p. 6.

in enabling bureaucracies to do their work efficiently – a matter on which there is much evidence. This can indeed be of central importance to the historian in studying particular societies and institutions and to the statesman in formulating policies. Eliminating corruption overnight in Thailand, Indonesia, the Philippines, the USSR or China is impossible, precisely because without it the present economy and administration would abruptly grind to a halt and the cooperation and accommodation necessary for their operation would disintegrate.

Further, as both Robert Merton and Philip Selznick have pointed out, Weber's emphasis on precision and reliability in administration, on its rule-bound character, has to be supplemented by a recognition that human attitudes and relationships are involved. The norms of impersonality may bring administrators into conflict with citizens and thus make them 'inefficient'. Functional sub-division will set up sub-group loyalties in the bureaucracy vital to the successful functioning of the sub-division, yet leading to conflicts within the whole.[5] That point is more damaging to Weber's theory. It brings out one of the general difficulties of functional social theories and of the concept of ideal types. That which is 'functional', 'efficient', is not always a coherent logical structure – efficiency may depend, and usually does, on a delicate balancing, in concrete contexts, of competing and conflicting trends and *desiderata*. A bureaucracy needs both impersonality and 'good relations', predictability and flexibility, rules and discretions, central control and local initiative. Weber's ideal-type bureaucracy, as a theoretical construct, is not undermined by this. Only by formulating that construct can we see both the extent to which actual bureaucracies depart from it and when and why they do so functionally or dysfunctionally. But when and why this is so we cannot determine in the abstract – we must look at actual bureaucratic institutions and the societies in which they work, at the character of the population, at the technologies available, at ideologies and traditions. Neither in the attempt to understand history nor in the attempt to formulate

5 Robert K. Merton, 'Bureaucratic Structure and Personality', *Social Forces*, vol. XVII, 1940, pp. 560–8, reprinted with minor modifications in Robert K. Merton et al., eds, *Reader in Bureaucracy*, Glencoe, Ill., 1952, pp. 361–71, and Philip Selznick, *TVA and the Grassroots*, New York, 1966, and, in an earlier version, 'An Approach to a Theory of Bureaucracy', *American Sociological Review*, vol. 8, 1943, pp. 47–54. Cf. Albrow, op. cit., p. 65.

administrative and political principles for our own age can we work from general abstract principles alone.

Weber captured an important element in the development of modern conceptions of bureaucracy as a 'public service' when he stressed that a bureaucracy should be a staff carrying out policies given to it. That aspect of bureaucracy – the extent to which it influences policies, ignores them or creates its own – has long caused concern and causes more concern as the scale and complexity of administration increase. In recent writing, there has been greater emphasis on and recognition of the relationship of particular functional departments in the bureaucracy with 'clients' and others who form an interest group in society. The latter may seek, honestly or corruptly, to turn that section of the bureaucracy into their 'representatives'. The relevant section of the bureaucracy may even play that role on its own initiative, as a result of its work experience and compete, on behalf of its 'clients', with other sections of the bureaucracy, seeking to alter the allocation of resources, the nature and application of rules and even the overall policies. It is difficult to see bureaucracies as playing an important role in 'feedback' without giving at least limited endorsement to such internal bureaucratic initiatives. When sections of bureaucracy 'go public', the question becomes more difficult, though it was long a socialist demand (in countries not governed by socialists) that public servants should be free to speak out and oppose policies they were expected to administer. Even in ancient China, there were acceptable ways of doing this under penalty – by committing suicide to impress on the emperor how serious an issue had been dismissed.

On this basis, we are in a position to consider Weber's ideal type of bureaucracy as a tool for giving us new or at least fruitful perspectives on the past and for coping with modern developments, especially in post-industrial technologically highly advanced societies. When it comes to the past it could be argued that Weber, by focusing on the contrast between traditional and rational–legal authority and legitimation, has overemphasized the break between aspects of bureaucratic theory and practice in the great bureaucracies of ancient societies and those of the modern age – though it is also precisely through his ideal type that he is able to bring out reasons for the instability of many ancient bureaucracies and patterns of rule.

Weber's work itself did much to draw attention to the power and size of hierarchically organized formal administrative structures in parts of the ancient world. It would be perverse not to use the terms 'bureaucracy' and 'bureaucracies' for organized administration through others on that scale. It would also be important not to confuse officials with local notables or feudal lords, deriving some authority from the king but not all of it and performing some tasks and passing on some tribute or taxes to him. Weber was right in arguing that in ancient and medieval societies the line between an official and a comparatively independent magnate or lord accepting some duties to and control by the state could be uncertain. Often, however, the uncertainty is ours and stems from the fact that we do not know enough. The line, as Weber said, can easily be crossed when the centre is weak or parsimonious, when it leaves officials to raise their own reward. But Weber did systematically underestimate the extent to which 'rational' bureaucratic procedures were developing even in very early times.

There is some basis, then, for speaking of bureaucracy in (parts of) the ancient world, for noting that it is more unstable in some societies than others and for describing societies like post-Han China as highly bureaucratized. We can make sense of the notion that there are more bureaucratized societies and less bureaucratized societies, as well as societies that have no significant bureaucratic structures at all. The Marxist concept of the Asiatic mode of production recognized, correctly, that there were societies in which the state – the ruler and the officials acting in his name – organized and controlled production, distribution and exchange on a national scale, appropriating the 'surplus value' produced by the labour of the people to such extent that the state formed the Marxist ruling and exploiting class. In such societies, power *vis-à-vis* 'the masses' rested principally upon state-created or state-recognized position, not on wealth or status independent of the ruler. The parallel between those societies and the modern communist states is striking and has struck many; it is fair to say that both kinds are examples of bureaucratic societies. To say this is to say that they are ruled by state officials that form a self-perpetuating bureaucracy which confront the people as the privileged and ruling class. It is not to say that the emperor, king or general secretary is a mere puppet of this class. That suggestion may and does raise complex and difficult issues that cannot be decided on general theoretical or sociological principles. Nor is it easy to characterize the social origins and composition of such bureaucracies as independent variables.

In speaking of bureaucratic or bureaucratized societies, we are using a comparative, relative standard – plotting points on a continuum. The western world today seems increasingly bureaucratized to most of its inhabitants. It would not seem very bureaucratic to a Chinese or a Russian of almost any historical period. The movement represented by Gorbachev and Deng Xiao-ping contributes a conscious if limited attempt to de-bureaucratize their own societies precisely in the sense of weakening the scope and unassailability of bureaucratic control, of control by officials and official procedures.

To speak of bureaucratic societies is to speak of the role and relative power and importance of officials serving or constituting the state. Turning to Weber's narrower and more specific conception of modern rational bureaucracy as an ideal type, one might argue that he did grasp an important historical trend. Sir Ernest Barker called it 'the disengagement of the state', the creation of a public as opposed to a royal service. Weber also saw some of the most important causes of instability in pre-modern bureaucracies – the tendency to convert offices into fiefs. But his concept of 'rational' bureaucracy as an ideal type brings together, into an allegedly logical relationship, features of modern bureaucracies that can and do come into conflict with each other or become dysfunctional in changed social circumstances. Thus in modern, post-industrial societies – where we have a great tendency to elevate the newspaper headlines of the decade into the truth of the century – there are nevertheless features Weber took insufficient notice of. The increasing prosperity, education and sophistication of the population in the fortunate post-industrial societies have, as many socialists predicted, led to a steady diminution of the role of direct physical force in the allocation of goods and of direct authoritarian command in the production of goods and administration of services. The computer has meant a drastic reduction in the labour necessary to assemble as a matter of routine the information on which bureaucracies work. The increasing education and sophistication of the workforce has led to more collaborative and cooperative styles of work. The rigidity of centralized direction, in a world of increasing complexity and of much greater public protest and scrutiny, has proved even more dysfunctional than it was 100 years ago. Telephone exchanges, as one study proved, operated more efficiently if the operators felt themselves to be working in a significant area of personal discretion and responsibility, provided that area is not too great. As bureaucracies grow in size and intrude into more and more aspects of social life, functional specialization reveals some of its dangers. Centralized direction as the imposition of a system of general rules comes to have greater and greater difficulty in dealing not only with special cases, but with particular areas of concern, particular classes of people, particular and often transitional problems. For the practising administrator and the administrative theorist, less so for the historian, these questions of balance can become central. They do so especially in a society of rapid change, where flexibility and innovative responsiveness to change suddenly appear more crucial even than stability and obedience to rules. One result of this is a movement away from the legal education that had been replacing the generalist training of administrators toward ever more specialized training for lower and middle level bureaucrats and the elevation of economic and scientific training at the top. Another movement, linked with demands for wide-ranging social reform on single but pervasive issues (such as the position of women, of the poor, of indigenous peoples) has been the formation of political-administrative task forces criticizing and 'making inputs' into the work of many ministries rather than seeking a ministry or department of their own, so as to draw attention to the unexpected impact on women or the poor, or indigenous peoples, of policies not on the face of it related to those issues. Together with these demands for wide-ranging and rapid social reform have come far-reaching attacks on or rejections of the ideal of bureaucratic impartiality and of the separation between the political formulation of policies and the administrative implementation of them. All this, very visibly, undermines Weber's elevation of ideal-type bureaucracy as 'rational', in the sense of desirable, for modern conditions. But it does not, I believe, undermine it as a tool for understanding the changes in modern life and the attacks on it. Nor could the present elevation of other concerns make sense if the stable structures and rules, the bureaucratic efficiency and impersonality of the past could not be taken for granted. In fact, however, efficiency and impersonality cannot be achieved or maintained as a basic, necessary and desirable foundation for administrative work and discretionary decisions without continued emphasis on the features Weber treated as characterizing 'rational' ideal type bureaucracy. The point is not to get rid of that concept or of that type of administrative integrity and impersonality but to recognize competing requirements and *desiderata*. Some of the new public concerns mentioned above, the demands for rapid social reform, have undermined and continue to undermine some of the virtues of 'rational' bureaucracy and the professional integrity of the bureaucrat as an impersonal administrator, putting aside his or her prejudices and predilections. A politicization of the public service that prevents it from acting as a brake on political wilfulness and arrogance can be the result. Here, too, it is a question of balance. The horrors of National Socialist Germany and other horrors have made people today extremely aware of the fact that unjust laws arc not made better by being justly administered and that they are made worse in their effects by being efficiently administered. The result has been a strong, perhaps excessive, revolt against rule-boundedness analogous to the belief that there is nothing between wearing jackboots and having bare feet. Neither extreme makes for a tolerable or a fair society.

With the spread of social egalitarianism, resentment of bureaucracy has indeed focused on rules and procedures, on bureaucratization even more than on bureaucrats. The resentment, often justified, is of the distortion of facts, values and activities in the interest of making them quantifiable, categorizable and more easily administered – though there is also the less worthy resentment of considerations that take account of interests other than one's own. There is the clash, noted by Daniel Bell, between an economic system that elevates efficiency, a political system that elevates equality and an educational and ideological trend that elevates self-determination. Here, bureaucracy as state organization has been very significantly supplemented by the increasing bureaucratization of the non-state sector, including corporations, trade unions, hospitals and schools (whether public or private). Weber himself stimulated considerable work, especially in Germany, on non-state bureaucracies and comparisons of these with those of the state. More recently, there has been much greater intertwining of public and private economic activity and services. The distinctiveness of the sphere assigned to the state and consequently to the public service has been greatly weakened and much of the western world has followed America in seeing no real distinction between the managerial skills and philosophies required in higher level public service and those required in the private sector. That does assault, to a significant degree, both the contemporary public servant's sense of vocation and career structure and permanence. It may bring other benefits, such as more direct responsiveness to 'market' and popular demands and greater flexibility in meeting these. But it is weakening both the dedication and the disinterestedness of those who saw the public service career as being just that – public service. The fact that 'disinterestedness' has become, in many circles, a dirty word, is not wholly to be welcomed.

A theoretical difficulty for Weber that has become especially evident in recent times is Weber's conflation of professional and administrative expertise – a source of conflict elevated by Talcott Parsons and Alvin Gouldner who see important tensions between the professional ethos and the administrative. More recently, Robert Brown,[6] drawing on a vast literature, has emphasized that bureaucratic administration, whether public or private, is nowhere near as stable in its self-maintenance as Weber believed, even when it is on Weber's criterion 'rational'. Brown cites W.G. Bennis[7] to bring out four major contemporary threats to a Weberian model of centralized bureaucratic administration built on routine work-flows, a pyramidal chain of command and a clear system of rules. These are rapid and unexpected change (now more and more frequent); an increase in size beyond sustainable growth; an increasing variety of specialized skills that replace the previous mass of simple repetitive jobs; an increasing demand

6 Robert Brown, 'Bureaucracy: the Utility of a Concept', in E. Kamenka and M. Krygier, eds, *Bureaucracy: The Career of a Concept*, London, 1979, pp. 135–55. I have also benefited, in considering modern bureaucracy, from some very perceptive comments from Peter Self.

7 W.G. Bennis, 'The Coming Death of Bureaucracy', in A.G. Athos and K.E. Coffey, eds, *Behavior in Organizations: A Multidimensional View*, Englewood Cliffs, NJ, 1968, pp. 256–66, cited by Brown, op. cit., pp. 147–8.

from the workforce that the tasks themselves be made more satisfying.

P.M. Blau and M.W. Meyer have suggested that in modern administrative structures the codes and procedures by which administrators work are increasingly 'subject to challenge, review and change. The bureaucratic hierarchy becomes a network for channeling information and appeals for review. Thus, managerial authority still exists in the organization, but it is depersonalized, being exercised not so much through issuing commands and close supervision as through designing effective impersonal control systems.'[8] As machines, especially the computer, supply more and more of the information, the role of direct interpersonal command diminishes, the number and importance of competent specialists consulted by colleagues and superiors increase and work becomes more cooperative. As Brown puts it, 'labour specialization, job rules, standard operating procedures, impersonal relations, and especially hierarchical authority, all limit variation, both of input and output'.[9] Bureaucracies may well divide into task-forces of temporary teams with minimum supporting staff and an extended family of interconnected computers and automated machinery dealing with large routine flows of work and requiring only a skeleton staff of overseers. This, though even now not beyond possibility, may take time to spread through the system. In the meantime, the number of task-forces – whether they are called that or not – constantly increases, as does the rapidity with which their members are expected to turn from one major task to another. The old concept of bureaucracy as requiring caution, rigidity and immersion in dull and safe routine is already becoming increasingly inapposite in modern societies of rapid social, political and technetronic change. So is the simple division between political rule and administrative service or between 'expert' advice and administrative responsibilities. It is here that *Gesellschaft* traditions of private law, freedom of speech, publication and information and effective democratic government remain the important, if imperfect, effective limitation on the power of bureaucrats and of bureaucracy *vis-à-vis* its clients, just as bureaucrats, with experts

8 P.M. Blau and M.W. Meyer, *Bureaucracy and Modern Society*, 2nd edn, New York, 1971, p. 143, cited by Brown, op. cit., p. 148.

9 Brown, op. cit., p. 153.

and academics, still offer some check on political dishonesty and shallowness, on frank appeals to self-interest and on the contemporary politician's preference for looking good in the short term in the media and in the marginal seat. The great crimes of history have been committed in the name of religion, of morality and of politics – not of bureaucracy.

This book, then, is to a significant extent a defence of Weber as the proposer of themes around which the historical study and understanding of bureaucracies can be organized. It is not a defence of Weber as someone who has exhausted the issues with which bureaucracies are confronted and which are relevant to understanding their organization and style of work. Those issues, as Weber himself saw, have to be dealt with concretely, in specific and changing historical and social contexts. Some of the criticism of Weber is an elaboration of this. More of it, today, is an emotional rejection of actual historical facts and trends – of the triumph of nation-states over stateless communities, of complexity over simplicity, of planning over taking it easy, of exercising authority over harming no one, or of western rationalism over backward-looking traditionalism and fundamentalism. Here, too, actual societies depend on a delicate and subtle balance between all of these – a balance that cannot be prescribed on the basis of general moral or political principles, and that necessarily changes with time.

A striking feature of the modern age is its greatly expanded experience of different modes of living and social organization and its increased recognition of complexity, of the possibility of handling different things in different ways, as well as its yearning for seemingly incompatible 'life-styles'. Let us return to a distinction we have made in the course of this book between *Gemeinschaft, Gesellschaft* and bureaucratic-administrative structures, institutions and *Weltanschauungen*. These terms should not be seen as designating whole societies or whole periods of human history. They should be seen, rather, as coexisting, competing and conflicting trends that have manifested themselves in human history, and in particular social institutions, including actual bureaucracies, themselves. *Gemeinschaft* elevates the spontaneous cooperation and common interest of a community based on interpersonal relations and shared outlook, ideology and tradition. On a wider scale, however, its 'social cement' has tended to be provided by imposed ideologies and social hierarchies. *Gesellschaft* elevates individual rights and pursuits in a framework of stable impersonal laws that see citizens as standing, legally and politically, in a horizontal relationship of equality and equivalence, having rights against the state and its officers in exactly the same way as the state and its officers have rights against them. Its formal equality can hide, or even facilitate, much substantive inequality – though it is on *Gesellschaft* ideology that the demand for substantive equality has fed. The bureaucratic-administrative elevates social purposes and social areas as planning goals. It sees the relationship between these goals and both functionaries and citizens as vertical relationships of subordination and sub-subordination. Ideally, it assigns to people a place in an administered society and an administered activity, even if the administration is ultimately for the good of the people. In spite of Weber's typically continental conflation of the two, it elevates administration, regulation, 'public' law concerned with ordering activities, rather than 'private' law, which is concerned with the rights of the parties before the court, which treats the state itself, in any particular case, as just another party and the social interest as just another (somewhat suspect) particular interest, sometimes (but only sometimes) overriding.

Gemeinschaft and *Gesellschaft* have been presented as direct conceptually systematic contradictories fighting each other on every point – though Edward Shils has correctly pointed out that the modern *Gesellschaft* is bearable only because it is palliated by the existence of innumerable *Gemeinschaften* within it. Others have stressed the strength of contractual reciprocities, and of economic dependence and self-interest, even within rural or tribal *Gemeinschaften*. The bureaucratic-administrative stands in a more complex relationship to each of these two opposites. It shares with the *Gemeinschaft* the elevation of the social against the individual, of responsibilities against rights, of common purposes against individual satisfactions, of specific response to social 'needs' against abstract rules designed to protect individuals. Both *Gemeinschaft* and the bureaucratic-administrative emphasize social relationships and the needs of social activities and provinces against the individual. They thus tend to reject the conception of the abstract individual, to define the administrator and the citizen as belonging to a certain group, as having a status – whether as pensioner, 'disadvantaged person', the 'prescribed authority', or whatever. Against the *Gemeinschaft*, however, the bureaucratic-administrative and the *Gesellschaft* share the elevation of law, rules and regularized procedures, the concepts of *intra* and *ultra vires* and the depersonalization of claims and demands.

Elsewhere,[10] Professor Tay and I have explored the contradictory tensions in socialism and in modern communist societies by arguing that traditional socialism stands in an ambiguous critical relationship to the *Gesellschaft* of *laissez-faire* capitalism, elevating *Gemeinschaft* criticisms and longings on the one hand and bureaucratic-administrative ones on the other. What was true of nineteenth-century socialism and modern communism has remained true, only more obviously so, as political climates and economic demands and arrangements change. But it has become equally true of modern western societies, even if the relative strengths of the three components differ. Modern western society has witnessed, simultaneously, a concerted attack on and subversion of the last remaining traditional status-bound *Gemeinschaft* institutions in that society – the family, the school, the university, the professions – in the interests of the *Gesellschaft* values of equality and de-traditionalization and of bureaucratic-administrative values of 'economic rationalization' and the reducing of all to a common administrative measure. Here 'bureaucratization' rather than 'bureaucrats' is the enemy. Here, as Weber foresaw, collegiality gives way to centralized control, pluralism to the monocratic principle and to corporatism, to what the Nazis called *Gleichschaltung,* making everything operate as part of a *unified* system. But we have also seen, simultaneously, an elevation of selected individual rights against both bureaucracies and *Gemeinschaft* institutions, an elevation of social planning and economic rationalization against individual rights and liberties and social differentiation, and a highly politicized elevation of 'community' values, participation and support.

While there is much strident overemphasis by partisan supporters of each course, there is, in practice at least, growing

10 See the contributions by A.E.-S. Tay and E. Kamenka in Kamenka and R.S. Neale, eds, *Feudalism, Capitalism and Beyond*, Canberra, London, 1975, pp. 126–44, and Kamenka and Tay, eds, *Law and Social Control*, London, 1980, pp. 3–26, 105–16.

recognition that *Gemeinschaft*, *Gesellschaft* and the bureaucratic-administrative all have their part to play in social life. This is so not only in the wider society as a whole, but within the public or civil service, and other bureaucratic institutions. There lip-service, at least, is increasingly paid to *all* of these ideals and styles of working. In practice we now have the search for an optimal mix, which cannot be deduced from general principles. But we search in the context of ever-increasing bureaucratization in practice on the one hand, of ever-increasing politicization (often dishonest) on the other, and of some fundamental changes in the nature of bureaucratic structures themselves that depart from the traditional concept of the bureaucratic-administrative. That which explains the past need by no means necessarily point the way to the future. At present still, bureaucratization, more than bureaucracies, is one of the great dangers of modern life. Shallow, media-oriented politicization is another. Here, too, Weber and Tönnies and a mass of modern writing help us to see the resulting collisions as more than random accidents. Nor will such a typology make us jump in surprise when we find the Byzantine bureaucrat or the Chinese official conscious of at least some similar tensions and conflicts. That things are the same and not the same – *eadem sed aliter* – is still the motto of history and of life.

Suggested Reading

There is a vast and ever-growing literature on bureaucracy. This is especially so if one takes into account such relevant concerns as the history and practice of public administration and business management, organization theory, executive government, the 'trustification' of firms and growth of corporations, the psychology and sociology of political and administrative structures and their members, changing economic and other roles of the state, problems of 'public choice', etc. Most books and articles that address 'bureaucracy' by that name have been written by political scientists, though there is now increasing participation and use of the term by sociologists, economists, historians and anthropologists. There is less historically conceptual and theoretical writing than one might have expected and rather less, too, in the way of general historical or comparative overviews, though the work of Max Weber and his characterizations still form a primary point of departure for analysis or criticism. Among political scientists, much of that criticism is behaviourist in tone, concerned, as H.D. Lasswell put it in the title of a famous book, with *Politics: Who gets What, When, How* (New York, 1936), or with bureaucratic structures as examples of complex interaction between people.

Readers of this volume seeking additional literature will have to decide early whether they wish to pursue their interest in bureaucracy as a general social phenomenon stretching back to antiquity or are interested only in bureaucracy as a problem in modern society. They may wish to turn to more analytical work, to particular studies of temporal periods, countries and regions or to special aspects and problems. The bulk of writing on bureaucracy is on bureaucracy in the modern world, even in the twentieth century. Its earlier history has been left largely to historians of public administration or of the growth and vicissitudes of state power. There is substantial literature of this sort on

China, Prussia and Russia, where bureaucracies stood at the centre of public affairs and where historians have been, as a result, more interested in bureaucracy as a social category.

The reader seeking a broad introduction to the modern concept of bureaucracy and to nineteenth- and twentieth-century attitudes to bureaucracy could do worse than begin with Martin Albrow's short but very intelligent contribution to the 'Key Concepts in Political Science' series, his *Bureaucracy*, London, 1970. Other lively and readable introductions to the subject include Michel Crozier, *The Bureaucratic Phenomenon*, Chicago, 1964; Guy Benveniste, *Bureaucracy*, San Francisco, 1977; Joseph La Palombara, ed., *Bureaucracy and Political Development*, Princeton, N.J., 1963; P.M. Blau and M.W. Meyer, *Bureaucracy in Modern Society*, 2nd edn, New York, 1971; Jan-Erik Lane, ed., *Bureaucracy and Public Choice*, London, 1987, and B. Guy Peters, *The Politics of Bureaucracy: A Comparative Perspective*, New York and London, 1978. From these books, the reader will gain an impression of the extent to which bureaucracy is a controversial subject, both in respect of its definition and its characteristics and in respect of its social effects.

A good overview and opportunity to sample late nineteenth- and earlier twentieth-century discussion of the many aspects of bureaucracy that would interest a political scientist can be gained from *Reader in Bureaucracy* edited by Robert K. Merton, Ailsa P. Gray, Barbara Hockey and Hannan C. Selvin, Glencoe, Ill., 1952. This book arranges its useful and important selections from leading writers under the headings 'Theoretical Conceptions', 'Bases for the Growth of Bureaucracy', 'Bureaucracy and Power Relations', 'The Structure of Bureaucracy', 'Recruitment and Advancement', 'The Bureaucrat', 'Social Pathologies of Bureaucracy' and 'Field Methods for the Study of Bureaucracy'. It contains an extensive if somewhat dated bibliography organized under these headings and also gives the reader a sense of the controversy that surrounds most of the relevant issues. E.N. Gladden's *A History of Public Administration*, vols I and II, London, 1972, traces and provides much factual information on public administration from the earliest times to the twentieth century in Europe, Asia and the Americas.

No student seriously interested in bureaucracy should go

further without reading the general account of bureaucracy, both patrimonial and modern rational-legal, in Max Weber, *Economy and Society: An Outline of Interpretative Sociology*, ed. Guenther Roth and Claus Wittich, 3 vols, New York, 1968. The most important sections on bureaucracy are in volume I and principally in volume III; numerous selections and truncated translations are available, including those edited by H.H. Gerth and C.W. Mills (*From Max Weber*, London, 1948 – see chapter VIII, 'Bureaucracy'), and Talcott Parsons (*The Theory of Social and Economic Organizations*, London, New York, 1947). Empirically-based criticisms of Weber, taking their departure from a case study of an American factory in the first instance and two public administration agencies in the second can be found in Alvin Gouldner, *Patterns of Industrial Bureaucracy*, Glencoe, Ill., 1954, and P.M. Blau, *The Dynamics of Bureaucracy*, revised edn, Chicago, 1963. Recent literature on Weber brings his political writings, especially his attitudes to parliament and government in Germany, and to socialism, into relation with his sociological work – see e.g., W.J. Mommsen, *The Age of Bureaucracy*, Oxford, 1974, *Max Weber and German Politics, 1890–1920*, Chicago, 1985, and his *Max Weber, Selections in Translation*, ed. W.G. Runciman, Cambridge, 1978. Other important classics in the discussion of bureaucracy both inspiring and supplementing Max Weber are Gaetano Mosca, *The Ruling Class* (first published in Italy, 1896), ed. and revised by A. Livingston, New York, 1939, and Robert Michels, *Political Parties* (first published in Germany, 1911), reprinted, New York, 1962.

Henri J.M. Claessen and Peter Skalník, eds, *The Early State*, The Hague, 1978, and *The Study of the State*, The Hague, 1981, provide a useful introduction, conscious of Karl Marx and the work of V. Gordon Childe, to recent discussion on the rise of states and state bureaucracies with the transition to stratified societies. S.N. Eisenstadt, *The Political Systems of Empires*, New York, 1963, carries the discussion further in time, in a more Weberian way, to the 'axial age', from about 1200 BC onward. For specific examinations of the state and bureaucratic government in the ancient Middle East and in Egypt, the reader will have to supplement these books with the standard works that put less emphasis on economic, political and administrative questions – at least until recently – than one might have expected. Cyril

Aldred, *The Egyptians*, London, 1961, and the Cambridge Histories of the Ancient World and of India make a useful starting point for reference. For ancient India, the student could also look at A.S. Altekar, *State and Government in Ancient India*, 2nd edn, rev. and enl. Banaras, 1955, H.N. Sinha, *The Development of Indian Polity*, Bombay, London and New York, 1963, and Narayan Chandra Bandyopadhyaya, *Of Hindu Polity and Political Theories* (first published 1927), ed. N.N. Bhattacharyya, Calcutta, 1980. *Kautalya's Arthasastra* has been published, under that title, in an English translation by R. Shamasastry, Mysore, 1961. For Mughal (Mogul) and British India, the reader could go on to Ibn Hasan, *The Central Structure of the Mughal Empire*, Oxford, 1936, and L.S.S. O'Malley, *The Indian Civil Service 1601–1930*, London, 1931. Here, too, there is a burgeoning specialist literature that is revolutionizing, or at least challenging, much past understanding of Indian history and of British India.

Bureaucracy in China figures in every serious history of the country. A reader who is not a sinologist will find most useful Wolfram Eberhard, *A History of China*, transl. E.W. Dickes, Berkeley and Los Angeles, 1950, the 'introductory orientations' in Joseph Needham, *Science and Civilisation in China*, vol. 1, Cambridge, 1954, Etienne Balazs, *Chinese Civilization and Bureaucracy: Variations on a Theme*, transl. H.M. Wright, New Haven, 1964, H.G. Creel, *The Origins of Statecraft in China*, vol. 1, Chicago, 1970 and Ch'ien Mu, *Traditional Government in Imperial China: A Critical Analysis*, transl. Chün-tu Hsüen and George O. Totten, Hong Kong, 1982. Max Weber's *Religion of China*, transl. and ed. by H.H. Gerth, Glencoe, Ill., 1951, is an important study, though based on inadequate knowledge. More detailed examinations include Hans Bielenstein, *The Bureaucracy of Han Times*, Cambridge, 1980, E.A. Kracke, *Civil Service in Early Sung China 960–1067*, Cambridge, Mass., 1953, and James T.C. Liu, *Reform in Sung China*, Cambridge, Mass., 1959, Charles O. Hucker, *The Censorial System of Ming China*, Stanford, 1966, and Wolfgang Franke, *The Reform and Abolition of the Traditional Chinese Examination System*, Cambridge, Mass., 1960.

Good introductions to the vast topic of Roman and Byzantine bureaucracies are Karl Loewenstein, *The Governance of Rome*, The Hague, 1973, and T.F. Carney, *Bureaucracy in Traditional*

Society: Romano-Byzantine Bureaucracies Viewed from Within, Lawrence, Kansas, 1971. Historians of Rome and Byzantium generally have long paid considerable attention to the structure of Roman administration; they do so even more now.

Literature on Islam, including Islam in Persia, Egypt and the Seljuk and Ottoman Empires, is also burgeoning, with important discussions of the nature of Islamic feudalism as a 'bureaucratic feudalism' playing a significant role. Albert Howe Lybyer, *The Government of the Ottoman Empire in the Time of Suleiman the Magnificent* (first published 1913), New York, 1966, constitutes a readable introduction. Material on Inca society and administration is surprisingly sparse, no doubt because the society was non-literate and the original written accounts compiled by their European conquerors more than sketchy and unreliable. Apart from literature in Spanish, based on accounts by conquistadores and early generations of Spanish priests in Peru, there are Louis Baudin, *L'Empire socialiste des Inka*, Paris, 1928, and his *Les Incas du Perou*, Paris, 1942, Sally F. Moore, *Power and Property in Inca Peru*, New York, 1958, and Geoffrey Conrad and Arthur A. Demarest, *Religion and Empire: The Dynamics of Inca and Aztec Expansionism*, Cambridge, 1984. Joseph A. Tainter, *The Collapse of Complex Societies*, Cambridge, 1988, surveys and draws attention to a substantial body of writing seeking to explain why various empires and state-centred administrative and political structures have collapsed.

Beginning with F. Engels, *The Origin of the Family, Private Property and the State* (numerous editions) and with Marx's references to the 'Asiatic mode of production', Marxists have had to face the problem of accounting for societies in which the state, rather than a class of property owners, appears to be the principal organizer of production, distribution and exchange and the appropriation of surplus value. Both the pre-history of this problem adumbrated in Aristotle and the subsequent treatment of it in seventeenth-, eighteenth- and nineteenth-century European thought, and by Marxists throughout the world, are discussed in Lawrence Krader, *The Asiatic Mode of Production*, Assen, 1975, Marian Sawer, *Marxism and the Question of the Asiatic Mode of Production*, The Hague, 1977, and Anne M. Bailey and Joseph R. Llobera, eds, *The Asiatic Mode of Production: Science and Politics*, London, 1981. The discussion, stretching back to the 1920s in Marxist circles, was given powerful impetus by Karl A. Wittfogel's polemical *Oriental Despotism: A Comparative Study of Total Power*, New Haven, 1957, which sets the Asiatic mode of production, or 'hydraulic' society, into a comparative and political context seeing in it the foundation of 'totalitarianism' in the ancient, medieval and modern world.

The development of public administration and bureaucratic structures in Europe has long been studied by historians. Walter Ullmann, *Principles of Government and Politics in the Middle Ages*, 2nd edn, London, 1966, sets out some of the important tensions and presuppositions of feudal society in Europe that helped to distinguish it from most other societies. Sir Ernest Barker, *The Development of Public Services in Western Europe 1660–1930*, London, 1945, and Herman Finer, *Theory and Practice of Modern Government*, London, 2nd edn rev., New York 1949, trace the emergence and consolidation of public functions and public services in Europe, while G.N. Clark, *The Seventeenth Century*, 2nd edn, Oxford, 1947, emphasizes their development throughout Europe under absolutism.

For England, T.F. Tout's *Chapters in The Administrative History of Mediaeval England*, 6 vols, Manchester, 1928–37, esp. vols 1 and 2 and *The Place of the Reign of Edward II in English History*, 2nd edn, rev., Manchester, 1937, traced the origins of royal administration, while G.R. Elton, *The Tudor Revolution in Government*, Cambridge, 1953, and G.E. Aylmer, *The King's Servants: The Civil Service of Charles I, 1625–1642*, New York, 1961, and *The State's Servants: The Civil Service of the English Republic 1642–1660*, London, 1973, together with W.J.M. McKenzie and J.W. Grove, *Central Administration in Britain*, London, 1957, are among books that carry the story further forward.

The work of the great German historians of public administration and administrative centralization, Otto Hintze and Gustav Schmoller, is continued in Reinhold August Dorwart, *The Administrative Reforms of Frederick William I of Prussia*, Cambridge, Mass., 1953, and Hans Rosenberg, *Bureaucracy, Aristocracy and Autocracy: The Prussian Experience 1660–1815*, Cambridge, Mass., 1958. G.S. Ford, *Stein and the Era of Reform in Prussia, 1807–1815*, Princeton, 1922, is of interest, so, more generally, are F.L. Carsten, *The Origins of Prussia*, Oxford,

1954, and Hajo Holborn, *A History of Modern Germany, vol 2: 1648–1840*, London, 1965.

French centralization of state functions has attracted an enormous literature, including much work on the Enlightenment, and distinguishing the aristocracy of the sword from the aristocracy of the robe, studying mercantilism, *intendants* and prefects as well as taxation and financial administration generally. To this James E. King, *Science and Rationalism in the Government of Louis XIV 1661–1683*, Baltimore, 1949, and Franklin L. Ford, *Robe and Sword: The Regrouping of the French Aristocracy after Louis XIV*, New York, 1968, and the work of Jacques Ellul, *Histoire des institutions,* 5 vols in 4 Paris, 1982–84, form lively and interesting introductions.

For Russia, too, there is an ever-growing literature. An initial approach could be made through G. Vernadsky, *A History of Russia*, 4th edn, New Haven, Conn., 1951, R. Pipes, *Russia Under the Old Regime*, London, 1974, and Walter McKenzie Pintner and Don Karl Rowney, eds, *Russian Officialdom: The Bureaucratization of Russian Society from the Seventeenth to the Twentieth Century*, London, 1980.

By the nineteenth century, functionaries, public servants, *chinovniki*, had become social types; some well-known literary portraits are to be found in Honoré de Balzac, *The Government Clerks* (*Les employés*), Charles Dickens, *Bleak House* and *Little Dorrit*, Nikolai Gogol, *The Government Inspector* (*Revizor*), Anthony Trollope, *The Three Clerks*. Franz Kafka's *The Castle* and *The Trial* launched the twentieth century on the nightmare of the anonymously bureaucratic state.

The twentieth century raised, specifically and urgently, all the problems of administration in an increasingly interventionist western state, faced with the mass delivery of services and supervision of rapidly expanding industries, as well as those of reconciling bureaucracy and democracy, evaluating the role of socialist governments and societies and understanding fascism, national socialism and other forms of authoritarianism. A.A. Berle and G.C. Means, *The Modern Corporation and Private Property*, New York, 1933, with its emphasis on the shift within modern corporations from the owner to the professional manager exercising control, helped to launch a new interest in 'managerial society' – a social formation that appeared to be neither capitalist nor socialist (Nazi Germany and Fascist Italy were thought to be examples by some, who linked their structure with that of the USSR under Stalin).

Leon Trotsky's *The Revolution Betrayed* (which stopped short of seeing bureaucratic deformation in the Soviet Union as a new social formation) was another source. The movement culminated in Bruno R[izzi], *La Bureaucratisation du monde*, Paris, 1939, Lucien Laurat, *Marxism and Democracy*, London, 1940 (French original, Paris, 1939) and James Burnham, *The Managerial Revolution or What is Happening in the World Now*, New York, 1941. Milovan Djilas, *The New Class*, first published in London, 1957, inaugurated a whole series of studies of Soviet and East European ruling elites and privileged classes as a 'new class'. Michael Vozlensky, *Nomenklatura: Anatomy of the Soviet Ruling Class*, transl. Eric Mosbacher, London, 1984, is one of the more recent works on this subject to emerge from the experience and research of Soviet dissidents, as does the more theoretical Andras Hegedus, *Socialism and Bureaucracy*, London, 1976.

Geoffrey K. Fry, *The Changing Civil Service*, London, 1985, is one of a host of books looking at public administration in the modern democratic world, while C.S. Hyneman, *Bureaucracy in a Democracy*, New York, 1950, Peter Self, *Administrative Theories and Politics*, 2nd edn, London, 1977, E.C. Page, *Political Authority and Bureaucratic Power*, Brighton, 1985, W.A. Niskanen, *Bureaucracy – Servant or Master*, London, 1973, and Eva Etzioni-Halevy, *Bureaucracy and Democracy: A Political Dilemma*, 2nd edn, London, 1983, take up the problems of limiting bureaucratic power.

Index